IDTRAVELLING

14 Days in Japan

First edition

ISBN: 978-1-9994579-0-7

This book was professionally typeset on Reedsy.
Find out more at reedsy.com

Contents

Prologue

A trip to JAPAN. It has been a dream of mine for the last five years. Finally, my husband, David and I got a chance to travel there in May of 2017. When we told our friends and family we planned to visit Japan, usually, we received a close variation of the same response, "Wow Japan! I have wanted to visit for a long time. I wish I can visit soon." This reply was more-or-less the same until we told one couple who visited Japan in 2016. During their trip, they have been to Tokyo and Mount Fuji for five days. They told us there was still so much they wanted to do there. So we agreed to go together during the "golden week" (I will talk about it later in the book).

It is always a bit of a risk to travel with someone else since everyone has varying ideas about what they want to get out of the trip. So before doing anything else, we first sat down with our friends, and each of us stated our expectations for the trip. We realized that we were all very interested in visiting Tokyo, Kyoto, and Osaka. We were intent on going to a hot spring and we also found out none of us was excited about museums. Lastly, and most importantly, we were excited about tasting the local cuisine. On these premises, I began my research on Japan.

Getting Ready

Starting my research on Japan was a big challenge. Where do I even begin? Japan is 3,008 km long and 1,645 km wide[1], with a population of more than 126.7 million and more than 2600 years of existence[2]. This amazing country seemed to me like a different planet altogether. I decided to start with the simplest tool: YouTube. I watched videos by *Mark Wiens*, *internationally ME*, *Experience JAPAN with YUKA*, and *Simon and Martina*. After watching these videos, I was very eager to go, but also extremely hungry! Japanese food looks so interesting and delicious; I might have gained weight only by watching these videos and snacking all the while.

When I learned about all the foods I wanted to try and some of the places I wanted to visit, I advanced my research to the following websites: *Japan-talk*, *Japan cheapo*, and *Japan-guide*.

We booked all our hotels long in advance since we didn't want to miss out on good deals.

Tip: We looked for hotels that are located close to major transportation terminals, like subways, and train stations. Staying in these locations helped us save time and walking energy since we did A LOT of walking anyways (13 km per day on average). While some websites[3] recommend booking hotels one month in advance, others[4] recommend booking as soon as possible for peak seasons and national holidays.

Good to Know: Japan is a cash country. Credit cards are not accepted everywhere. Moreover, not all ATMs accept foreign credit or debit cards[5].

Since Japan is a cash country, we came to Japan with enough cash for the whole trip. We calculated that we would need to take ¥400,000 Japanese Yen (JPY) with us (read the "Trip Budget" section to see how much we spent on accommodations, transportation, food, and attractions. This section can help you plan how much money you might need). It's worth mentioning that we already paid for some of the hotels and bus tickets in advance. Also, due to several unexpected purchases, we spent the entire budget before our last day was over. As a result, we had to withdraw some money on the last day of our trip. We used an ATM in a 7-Eleven store (they are very popular in Japan). Other locations with an ATM that accepts a foreign debit card include post offices and AEON supermarkets[6]. Some websites[7] claim the ATMs in Japan offer better exchange rates than banks in your home country, but it's better to check the rates for yourself.

If you decide to take cash with you, find out where you can exchange your money for the Japanese yen at least a month in advance since some places are required to purchase it from other suppliers. This process may take some time. Another possibility is to exchange your money at the airport, but the exchange rate is usually worse. We exchanged our money at the bank two months in advance because the rate was good and we wanted to be sure we would get the money in time. Also, since it was a large amount of money, we felt that it would be better for the exchange to occur in a safe place like a bank.

It took me about two months to research the Japanese culture, history, food, and travel destinations. The highlights of which I summarized, along with my trip destinations, comments, and tips, in the following chapters.

Sources:

[1] http://www.nationsencyclopedia.com/Asia-and-Oceania/Japan-LOCATION-SIZE-AND-EXTENT.html

[2] https://en.wikipedia.org/wiki/Japan

[3] https://www.hospitalitynet.org/news/4070411.html

[4] https://www.ricksteves.com/travel-tips/sleeping-eating/reserve-accommodations

[5] https://boutiquejapan.com/money-in-japan/

[6] https://www.jnto.go.jp/eng/basic-info/shopping/atms-2.html

[7] https://transferwise.com/gb/blog/atms-in-japan

1

Day 1: Getting to Tokyo

My husband, David and I took an Air Canada flight from Toronto Canada, with a connection in Vancouver. After almost 17 hours of travel, tired but excited, we arrived at the Tokyo Narita airport. We looked for the Skyliner train to Nippori station (which is located close to our hotel), but we were so overwhelmed by the number of people, signs, and trains. Fortunately, the information counter pointed us in the right direction. There are two great things about the Skyliner train. First, it takes only 40 minutes to get to Nippori. Second, it is above ground, and you can observe the rural parts outside of Tokyo.

We booked Hotel Lungwood (approx. ¥9,550 per night) in the Nippori neighborhood, which is conveniently located about four minutes walking distance from Nippori station, although it took us about 30 minutes to get to the hotel because we took the wrong exit from the station.

Tip: I highly recommend purchasing a data only SIM card[1] to be connected to the Internet and not rely only on Wi-Fi networks. The main advantage for us was the ability to use our phone for navigation: to know what subway line to take, and how to get to our destination. It saved us a lot of time. We purchased a SIM card later in our trip, but you can purchase it at the airport.

Tip: If you have navigation problems (like me), you can look at a station's floor plan online[2], provided by JR (Japan Railway Company). The floor plan can assist you in finding the correct exit.

Tip: It is a good idea to stay in a hotel close to a transportation station and to avoid a touristy neighborhood. We chose the Nippori area because it is mostly a residential neighborhood. Staying at a residential area allowed us to explore restaurants visited mainly by locals. These restaurants usually provide more authentic food than restaurants for tourists. Moreover, our hotel was located near Nippori station, which is a central station connected to several subway lines including the JR line.

Even though Nippori is mainly a residential neighborhood, it has a few tourist attractions, including the Yanaka cemetery, Nippori fabric town, and temples. According to *Japan-talk[3]*, most of the temples in Nippori were moved there from Edo (central Tokyo) during the 19th century. This relocation of temples was a precaution against fires. Unfortunately, we didn't have a chance to visit these destinations during our stay in Nippori, but the following paragraphs will provide some information for those interested.

The Yanaka cemetery is a 100,000 square meter cemetery that was established in 1872[4]. Before 1872, most cemeteries were the property of Buddhist temples. However, in 1872, Shinto funerals gained popularity and the government issued a new policy for separation between Buddhists and Shintoists. As a result, a public cemetery was established. In 1935, the cemetery was named Yanaka Reien (literally "Yanaka spirit park"). It is a popular spot for flower viewing in the spring (*hanami*)[5]. Hanami is an old Japanese tradition to welcome the spring and appreciate the beauty of nature. Not far from the Yanaka cemetery is another attraction: the Nippori fabric town. The Nippori fabric town is one kilometer long and contains about 100 stores[6].

Some of the shops give tourists a complimentary English map, which provides information about several of the shops in the area.

Our friends arrived in Tokyo three hours before us, and since we didn't have a SIM card yet, we arranged to meet in the hotel lobby. After putting our luggage in the hotel room, the four of us went to explore the local cuisine. We went to an *Izakaya* restaurant ( )[7] located two minutes away from the back entrance of the hotel, close to a Mos Burger branch. Izakaya is a Japanese pub with typically inexpensive small portions. The word "Izakaya" literally means, "stay in sake shop."[8] Izakaya is a favorite for both young and old since it is easy to find, cheap, and can accommodate big parties. About 20% of all the restaurants in Japan can be considered an Izakaya. The Izakaya we went to served *Yakitori*, a small skewer with meat or vegetables, or both. It is cooked over a charcoal grill, commonly using binchotan charcoal (white charcoal)[9]. Finding Yakitori in an Izakaya menu is very common.

The nice thing about going to an Izakaya is the open and lively atmosphere. When you enter the Izakaya, you will customarily be greeted by all the workers. The greeting gives a very pleasant feeling that you are welcome. The well-lit room, laughing people, and semi-open kitchen deepen this feeling and give the Izakaya a homey atmosphere.

The Izakaya we went to wasn't crowded and it was quiet enough to have a good conversation with friends. We were seated on floor seating cushions. The menu was in Japanese, but as luck would have it, it had pictures of the menu items. We ordered cherry tomato, green pepper, chicken breast, skin, liver, and hearts Yakitori. Also, we noticed most of the tables had a marinated mackerel dish. We assumed it was the house special and ordered it as well, along with some drinks.

Good to know: In an Izakaya, a customer is expected to order a food and drink item. It is considered rude not to order both[10].

First, we received an appetizer we did not order. It was a tiny salad-like dish we had a hard time identifying. It tasted like fish, but the waiter told us it was actually made of beans. Either way, it was very pleasant and left a taste for more. Later, we discovered that the appetizer is a Japanese custom called *Tsukidashi.*

Good to know: It is common for Japanese restaurants to serve an appetizer (*Tsukidashi).* Usually, the Tsukidashi is not free and you may see it on your bill as a "table charge."

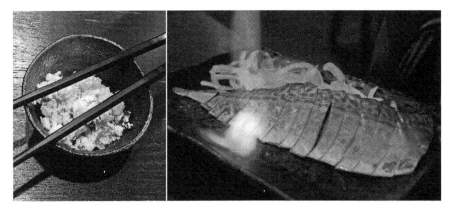

Left: bean salad Tsukidashi. Right: a torched mackerel.

All skewers were very good (except for the chicken skin. I am not a fan), but the chicken liver stood out. It was superb. It was the best chicken liver skewer I ate in Japan, or ever before. It was cut to almost identical small pieces and was cooked to perfection. Each bite melted in my mouth. Next, the waiter came with the mackerel dish in one hand and a torch in the other. He torched the skin of the mackerel until it was golden- brown and sizzling while we watched excited and hypnotized. The torched mackerel came with a thinly sliced onion topping, which compliment the salty fish nicely. I'm not a huge fan of mackerel, but I could appreciate the thought that went behind the dish.

We had some room left for additional menu testing, but we couldn't agree on what we wanted. Some of us wanted a beer with tempura and others preferred sashimi. Eventually, we decided to go to *Watami* restaurant, located close to Nippori station. The restaurant has a great variety on its menu and that is exactly what worried me. From my experience, usually, when you go to a restaurant, the menu has some theme. Here, it felt so disorganized and inconsistent, but it turned out to be exactly what we needed. Each portion we ordered was amazing. They probably had a lot of menu options because they are so good at making so many things.

We got a complimentary Tsukidashi egg salad, with ham, onion, and beans. We also ordered a beer and plum liqueur, along with tuna sashimi (raw tuna), grilled salmon belly nigiri, and *Gyoza*. Gyoza is a Japanese dumpling usually filled with pork meat, steamed and fried on one side until crispy brown. This process makes the meat inside very juicy, while the dough becomes slightly sweet from the frying. The salmon belly is a fatty piece that went well with the side rice, yet the star of the show was the tuna sashimi. It came with freshly grated wasabi and soy sauce. It was the perfect end to a very long day of travel and anticipation.

Good to know: It is not customary to leave a tip in a Japanese restaurant[11].

In the hotel room, we had time to examine the famous Japanese toilet. I'm not talking about the infamous old squat toilets that my friend likes to refer to as "hit-or-miss," I'm talking about the automated toilets. The interesting thing about them is how advanced they are. Common features include a seat warmer, and front and backwashing hoses. They have a control that contains many buttons that offer different functions. In fact, some of the toilets have more buttons than my car, which is also Japanese.

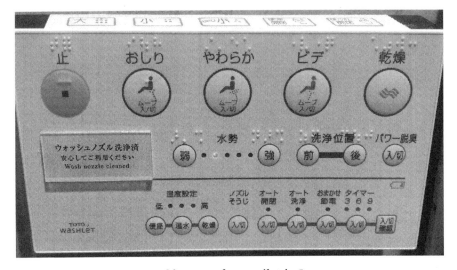

Control buttons for a toilet in Japan.

Good to know: It is up to you to decide whether you would use any of the additional functions the Japanese toilet provides. Either way, it is always good to know that means *stop*.

Sources:
[1] https://www.easygojapan.com/rental/en/news/info_prepaid-sim.html

[2] http://www.jreast.co.jp/e/stations/

[3] http://www.japan-talk.com/jt/new/nippori-in-tokyo

[4] https://en.wikipedia.org/wiki/Yanaka_Cemetery

[5] http://www.japan-talk.com/jt/new/nippori-in-tokyo

[6] http://metropolisjapan.com/nippori-textile-town

[7] https://r.gnavi.co.jp/e849999/

[8] http://www.japan-talk.com/jt/new/izakaya-japanese-pubs

[9] http://blog.chefsarmoury.com/2010/07/binchotan-japanese-white-charcoal/

[10]https://www.tripadvisor.ca/ShowTopic-g294232-i525-k10557342-Okay_to_eat_without_drinking_at_an_izakaya-Japan.html

[11] https://www.swaindestinations.com/blog/tipping-etiquette-when-traveling-in-japan/

2

Day 2: Shrine, Temple, and Fermented Oden

Morning came and with it our appetites. We went in search of a good place to have a Japanese breakfast near our hotel. We found a very nice restaurant located on the second floor of Hotel Sunny, called New Tokyo. The restaurant is roomy and has red covered seats embroidered with gold decorations. It offers a wide variety of breakfasts, from western style breakfasts to Japanese *bento boxes*. A bento box is a meal packed in a box, which originated during the Kamakura period (1185 to 1333) when cooked rice was developed[1]. Some bento boxes are packed in a way that features the food as a known animation character, scenery, or person.

Salmon bento box. In the background: New Tokyo restaurant seats.

We ordered two Japanese breakfast bento boxes: one that came with salmon and the other with mackerel. Both bento boxes had grated radish, rice, small savory pie, some beans, dried seaweed, and pickles. As in many places in Japan, the meal came with green tea and miso soup. It felt a little strange to have fish and rice for breakfast, but after the first bite, I forgot all about it. The most surprising part, though, was the savory pie, which turned out to be entirely soaked. When I took a bite from it, about half a cup of water spilled out. Thankfully, it didn't spill on my clothes. Don't get me wrong; the flavor wasn't half bad. When I was back home, I found out it was most likely *Ganmodoki*. Ganmodoki is a Japanese fritter made of tofu and vegetables and soaked in broth.

The traditional Japanese cuisine (*washoku*) is based on the principle that a meal should be visually aesthetic, and possess a variety of flavors, smells, and textures – all of which need to come together in harmony to provide a full sensory experience. Pickles, or *tsukemono*, are a necessary part of the Japanese meal since they are very colorful and provide a pungent contrast to the umami miso and the rice[2]. The rice is a staple food and a very important part of the Japanese culture, so much so that it used to be a currency in the past[3]. The miso soup

9

is the fermented soul food of Japan and can come as a side at breakfast, lunch, or dinner[4].

Japan has a wide selection of fermented foods. Some examples include miso, fermented fish and seafood, and pickles[5]. The wide variety of fermented items is made possible by the unique climate in Japan. The warm temperature and humidity provide the optimum conditions for the growth and reproduction of bacterial cultures, which contribute to the fermentation process. The fermentation process changes the texture and taste of food and increases its nutritional value. Fermented food is also believed to lower cholesterol, enhance the immune system, and help with digestion.

The only bad experience during our breakfast was the unpleasant smell of cigarettes inside the restaurant.

Good to know: Smoking is allowed in most restaurants and bars, and in some hotel rooms in Japan even though it is prohibited to smoke in the street. Smoking in the street is only allowed in designated smoking areas[6]. On the upside, there are currently campaigns for making Japan smoke-free by the Olympic games in 2020.

With renewed strength, we took the subway to Ueno station.

Tip: If you plan to use buses, subways, or JR trains, it is recommended to get a *Suica* card. It is a prepaid card that saves you the bother of purchasing tickets. Simply use a machine to charge money to your card. Go to the gate, tap the card on the machine and the fare will be automatically deducted from the card. Moreover, it allows you to pay for shopping in the station. This way, you can save time and eliminate the use of change.

A Suica card used at the subway station.

Good to know: A Suica card can be purchased at any JR (Japan Railways) station. The Suica card can be loaded and recharged (with up to ¥20,000) at any automatic ticket vending machine that displays the Suica logo[7]. The vending machine accepts only JPY (cash only). The card can be refunded at a ticket office, but only in the same region it was purchased. For example, if you purchased the card in Tokyo, it belongs to the Eastern region and can only be refunded in the East JR stations[8]. The Suica card can be used in subway stations in different JR regions. We got our card in Tokyo and used it in Tokyo, Kyoto, and Osaka.

Good to know: In Tokyo subway stations, you are typically expected to walk on the left side, unless there is a sign that tells you otherwise. It is important to try and follow this rule to avoid disturbing or bumping into people. This rule also applies outside the station.

Walking out of Ueno station from Shinobazu gate, we went to explore the stores around the station. Straight away, we noticed an extremely narrow building. Turns out it is not uncommon to see narrow buildings in major cities in Japan due to dense population and low availability of land for real estate[9]. A solution to these two problems is to build extremely narrow and high buildings to provide enough space on a very small lot size.

A narrow building close to Ueno station.

Real estate is not the only challenge arising from the dense population. Parking in Japan is also very challenging, but there are a few creative solutions to this problem. The solutions include automated parking, multi-level parking, and rotary entrance to a parking lot[10]. In the multi-level parking, the entire parking can move up or down to let new cars enter an available parking spot or leave the parking. This way, the parking footprint is much smaller than regular multi-level parking in a mall. The rotary entrance to a parking lot is a great solution to parking lots that don't have enough distance from the street, and therefore cars don't have enough space to make a turn and enter them. The rotary entrance is a circular platform that rotates cars 90 degrees for easy access into the parking lot.

Multi-level parking.

After admiring the building, we entered a nice store that sells every imaginable Canon camera. It's a great destination for photography enthusiasts. Close to it, there is a shop that was the reason behind our visit to Ueno. This shop sells prepaid data-only SIM cards. This is a great alternative to purchasing a travel plan from your mobile provider. We purchased a 2GB SIM card that is active for 30 days for ¥3,800. Finally, with an Internet connection, navigating the rest of our trip became much easier.

It is impossible to walk around in Japan and not notice the nationwide obsession with cuteness, or *Kawaii*. Kawaii started in the 1970s when mechanical pencils became available and schoolgirls began a trend of writing with cute rounded letters[11]. Although this new handwriting was banned in schools, it was adopted a decade later in magazines, comics, and advertising. Ultimately, new Kawaii merchandise, such as Hello Kitty was developed.

From left to right: a cute sign at the subway station, a Hello Kitty camera, and a Gashapon (vending machine) on the street near Ueno station.

The vending machine in the above image is called *Gashapon* which is a vending machine with a variety of toys in capsules. In each machine, there are several toys from the same series. The ball you receive is random and the concept is similar to that of Kinder Surprise.

We returned to the subway station where we saw a vending machine that sells coffee. Before our trip to Japan, we discovered there are vending machines in Japan that sell hot coffee in a can. My husband was very excited to try this cool concoction. He looked through the different coffee cans in the machine and he decided to buy a gold coffee can that had a flame drawing. He purchased it on the premise that a flame signified hot coffee, but he was wrong; the flame is a logo for Kirin's coffee.

Good to know: Warm drinks are either sold at a separate vending machine or have a sticker that says they are warm.

After we finished laughing at my husband and he drank his coffee, we headed towards the Kameido Tenjin Shrine. On the way to the shrine, we enjoyed the view of the skytree. The skytree is a radio and television broadcasting site and the tallest tower in Japan[12]. Kameido Tenjin shrine is a Shinto shrine and it is one of the most popular places to watch Wisteria blossom in Tokyo. The Wisteria usually starts to bloom in late April and continues until the first days of May. Although all the flowers and the original famous arched bridge burnt down during WWII, some date their origin to the Edo era and to the mid-1600s, respectively[13]. When we arrived, the bloom had already passed its peak. However, the blue sky, green pond, red bridge, and purple flowers gave the place a magical atmosphere.

Good to know: When visiting a shrine, behave calmly and respectfully. If you are sick, wounded, or in mourning, you should customarily not visit a shrine.

Good to know: Near the shrine is a purification fountain. You are supposed to take a ladle, fill it with water and rinse both hands. You are then expected to pour some water into your hand and transfer it to your mouth, rinse, and spit the water next to the fountain. You should not swallow the water[14].

Wisteria blossom at Kameido Tenjin Shrine.

The history of the Kameido Tenjin shrine dates back to the 9th century to Sugawara no Michizane, who was a scholar, poet, and eventually, a politician. During his political career, he was promoted by the Emperor Uda to the position of the Minister of the Right and a member of the Council-of-state. This promotion was done in an attempt to reduce the Fujiwara clan power over the government. The Fujiwara clan, the most powerful family during that period, was in control of many of the government areas. To remain in control, the clan accused Sugawara no Michizane of treason and he was exiled to the far southern Japanese island of Kyushu, where he died[15]. Soon after his death, a few disasters struck the capital (Kyoto) and the residents believed this was Sugawara no Michizane's revenge. After the disasters, Sugawara no Michizane was designated as Shinto's god of scholars, Tenjin. During the 17th century, a descendant of Sugawara no Michizane had a revelation in his dream where Sugawara no Michizane asked him to build him a shrine. In 1662, the Shogun Iyetsuna offered land for the proposed shrine and it was built later that same year[16]. Nowadays, you may find the 5-year-old Sugawara no Michizane's statue in the

Kameido Tenjin Shrine.

Kameido Tenjin Shrine.

One of the things I liked about going to shrines and temples in Japan is that you will most likely find food nearby. Many of the places we visited had a large variety of street foods in the area. This was also true for the Kameido Tenjin Shrine. Here, we tried sea snails and scallop skewers for ¥500 each. They were fresh, tasted decent, but a little too chewy for my taste. We also tried an amazingly delicious fried pastry filled with pork meat for ¥300. As a dessert, we got matcha ice cream in a cone. I'm not sure what was tastier, the ice cream or the cone. Either way, both were gone in two minutes.

Good to know: From our experience, street food is safe to eat. Generally, people often associate street food with poor hygiene. However, in Japan, this is not true. According to the Japan National Tourism

Organization (JNTO), the food and tap water in Japan are safe for consumption, including street food[17]. I am very sensitive to food, but in Japan, I did not have any problems despite eating a lot of street food.

The only downside to our tour of the Kameido Tenjin Shrine was that it was very crowded. We arrived in Japan during the golden week: a holiday that combines several holidays under one blanket. It is a very busy time in Japan since tourist attractions are packed and the hotels are completely booked. We chose to visit at this time for three reasons. First, it was a convenient time for our friends and us. Second, the weather at this time of the year is usually good in Japan, and third, we believed that during this time, Tokyo wouldn't be as busy as other cities since many families travel outside of Tokyo during this holiday. Unfortunately, we were wrong with this assumption, as Tokyo turned out to be full of tourists, and most attractions were very crowded. Then again, we don't know how it usually is.

Tip: If you want to avoid the golden week, check _online_ to find the exact dates. If you decide to travel during the golden week, plan your stay and book ahead.

Although most places were very crowded, we noticed the weather was very nice. During the daytime, it reached around 23 degrees Celsius and it seldom rained.

Good to know: The most popular times to visit Japan are in the spring, when the Sakura (cherry blossom) blooms, and the fall when Japan is covered in autumn colors. While these two seasons are indeed the most appealing times to visit Japan, the weather isn't at its best. We traveled at the beginning of May and the weather was perfect.

On our way back to the subway station, we entered a convenience store and bought a steamed bun filled with pork meat for ¥130. I wanted to try one of these since the first time I saw them on a YouTube video a few months back. I couldn't imagine the taste of a steamed bun and I thought it couldn't be as good as a freshly baked bun – I was wrong. The steamed dough was very soft and airy, while the pork meat inside was hot and juicy. A real delight!

We took the subway to Asakusa station, and on the way to Sensoji temple, we entered *Isomaru Suisan* restaurant for lunch. The restaurant has two floors and both were almost completely full. The host led us to a floor seating on the second floor. When we first saw the floor table, we were a little disappointed because it reminded us of the Izakaya we'd been to the previous day, where we also were seated on the floor. Although we were a young group, we all had leg and back pains seating on the floor for so long. Fortunately, in Isomaru Suisan, there was room under the table for our legs. Basically, you seat the same way you would on a chair, but on the floor.

The place had a very strong smoke smell and we noticed most tables had grills on them. Some of the portions come with a grill, so you have a nice dining experience of preparing your own food. We got a tablet with the menu on it and we ordered seafood kimchi, crab miso, and salmon sashimi with salmon roe on top. You can't go wrong with salmon sashimi with salmon roe, but I would also recommend trying the seafood kimchi and crab miso. The seafood kimchi is a unique mix of small cut sashimi and somewhat spicy kimchi with an egg yolk on top. The crab miso is essentially a creamy crabmeat with miso, topped with green onion slices, inside a crab shell. The crab comes with the grill and you heat it until this crab shell full of goodness sizzles. It was both delicious and pleasing to the eye. Also, the built-up expectation while you grill it is an added bonus.

Left: seafood kimchi. Right: crab miso at Isomaru Suisan restaurant.

The only negative part was that the waiter forgot to bring us one item we ordered, probably because the restaurant was so busy. In any case, we were full and happy when we left.

Good to know: Many restaurants provide a warm steamed towel called *Oshibori* to clean your hands before the meal (some places hand out cold *Oshibori* during the summer). To comply with Japanese etiquette, you should not use the *Oshibori* to wipe the sweat off your face. When you finish cleaning your hands, fold the towel nicely and leave it on the table until the end of the meal so you can wipe your hands once more, on the opposite side of the towel[18].

We left the restaurant and continued our journey to the Sensoji temple, also known as the Asakusa Kannon Temple. The Sensoji temple is the oldest temple in Tokyo and it dates back to the 7th century. Legend says that in 628 AD, the brothers Hinokuma Hamanari and Takenari went fishing and caught a statue of the Buddhist deity Kannon. Each time they put the statue back into the river, it came back to them and they decided to keep the statue[19]. When they returned from their fishing trip, they showed it to Haji no Nakatomo (a devoted Buddhist). Haji no Nakatomo recognized the statue's significance and built the

Sensoji temple for it.

Sensoji temple.

On the way leading to the temple, there is a 200-meter shopping street called *Nakamise[20].*

Good to know: Considering Sensoji temple is the oldest temple in Tokyo, it attracts many tourists, both foreign and Japanese. Therefore, it is very crowded at peak hours (during holidays and weekends)[21].

Souvenir sweets sold at the shopping street leading to Sensoji temple.

As was mentioned earlier, we arrived during the golden week. In other words, the place was completely packed. There were so many people, shops, and things to see that after five minutes of entering the *Nakamise* street, we lost sight of my husband. All of us had a phone with us, and still, it took us 30 minutes to locate him.

Tip: Prepare for crowded situations in advance. Create a system in case someone gets lost, such as going back to a known location.

When we finally found my husband, we were able to focus on other things like how amazing the weather was. It was sunny but not hot, with a light breeze, perfect for visiting this beautiful temple. The sun rays and the light breeze gave a picturesque look to the fake Sakura trees located near the temple. Another thing we saw next to the temple was burning incense. Incense is a very important part of Buddhism and is used to purify the space. Many people who visit the temple wave the incense smoke onto themselves. They do it to cleanse themselves, but also because it's believed that the incense smoke possesses a healing power[22].

Incense smoke at Sensoji temple.

Good to know: When visiting a temple in Japan, it is important to behave calmly and respectfully. If you go inside the temple, you'll need to take off your shoes.

Good to know: If you plan to light incense at a temple, put the flame out by waving your hand, not by blowing on it.

Walking around the temple, you may hear a rattling sound. If you follow the sound, you'll reach an attraction where you can get a fortune-telling paper strip called *Omikuji*. To get your own Omikuji, put a donation in the donation box, then shake a big metal tin, flip it, and shake until a stick with a number falls out. Go to the drawer indicated by the stick, and there, you'll find your fortune. If it's a good fortune, you are supposed to keep the strip in your wallet for a year. Otherwise, you are supposed to tie it to a post so the bad fortune won't come true[23].

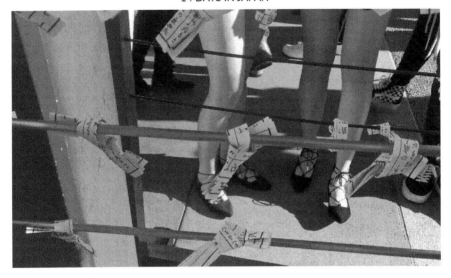

Omikuji notes predicting bad fortune, tied to posts at Sensoji temple.

Very close to the Omikuji, there are food vendors with a variety of street food. There, we tried a big crab leg on a stick for an affordable ¥500. It was topped with some mayonnaise and dried seaweeds. Yummy!

The difference between a temple and a shrine is that temples are dedicated to Buddha, while shrines are dedicated to a Shinto god. One way to distinguish between them is that a shrine will have a big traditional gate (called *Torii*), whereas a temple will have a Pagoda or a Buddhist deity[24].

Japan has two main religions: Buddhism and Shinto. Compared to Shinto (which is as old as the Japanese culture), Buddhism is relatively new in Japan. It was adopted during the 6th-century and for the most part, there were no conflicts between the two religions[25]. Furthermore, some Japanese people consider themselves to belong to both Shinto and Buddhism.

Six minutes walk from Sensoji temple, we stopped by a traditional crafts museum, named the Edo Downtown Traditional Crafts Center.

The entrance is free and it showcases art, crafts, lanterns, dolls, replicas of temples and shrines, and more. In addition to the nice crafts, the quiet, air-conditioned space provided a nice relief from the warm, sunny day.

Beautiful crafts at the Edo Downtown Traditional Crafts Center.

For dinner, we went to *Otafuku* restaurant. This establishment has been open and running since 1916 and is known for its *oden*. Oden is a warm dish that includes many different ingredients simmered in a broth. Each ingredient is ordered by the piece and is served inside the broth. The interesting thing about this specific oden restaurant is that it hadn't changed its broth for over 70 years! Ingredients are consistently being added to the broth. Every evening, the broth is moved to a different container, the pot is thoroughly cleaned, and the broth is poured back. This unique method gives the oden a somewhat fermented flavor that makes Otafuku stand out[26].

In Otafuku, we ordered two shrimp cutlets, quail eggs, and one meaty skewer. It was served with a lot of the delicious broth for a total of ¥2,350. We liked it so much (especially the broth) that the dish was empty by the time the waiter came back to check on us.

The entrance to Otafuku restaurant.

Next, we headed towards our hotel. On the way, we passed by a grocery store with a sign saying it is a tax-free shop for foreign visitors. When we got to the shop, we didn't know that the tax-free exemption is only applied to purchases above ¥5,000 (excluding tax). Consequently, we got a bunch of souvenirs and KitKats for a total of about ¥4,000. After the cashier informed us of this caveat, we spent 15 more minutes looking for more things to buy, and we reached and surpassed our goal. Pleased with ourselves, we went back to the same cashier. She calculated the new total and told us we qualified for the exemption, but first, we needed to give her one of our passports. Without thinking, I gave her my passport and the next thing I know, she stapled the receipt inside and stamped it. Afterwards, she took out duty-free bags and sealed everything inside. The sad thing about this was, my passport was brand new, while my husband's passport was going to be renewed soon.

Good to know: Many items sold in Japan (e.g., in stores) display a price tag that doesn't include a tax. When you purchase an item, the tax will be added to the bill. During our trip, the tax was 8%.

Good to know: After purchasing items using a tax-free exemption, you mustn't open the bags as long as you are in Japan, and you must have the bags and receipt with you at the airport before leaving Japan. When at the airport, you should show the receipt at the customs counter. For full details about tax-free shopping in Japan visit: http://tax-freeshop.jnto.go.jp/eng/shopping-guide.php

We returned to the hotel to put the shopping bags in our rooms and take a short break. After resting, we went to a restaurant near our hotel called *Tempura Tendon Tenya*. Tempura is deep fried battered fish, seafood, or vegetable. It is now a Japanese staple although it originated in Portugal. In 1543, Japanese and Portuguese relations began when a Chinese ship boarding three Portuguese sailors headed to Macau, accidentally arrived at the Japanese island of Tanegashima[27]. This accidental encounter led to the development of trading relations between Japan and Portugal in the following century. During this time, the Japanese became familiar with a Portuguese dish called *peixinhos da horta*. Peixinhos da horta are deep fried battered green beans. Later, this dish was adopted by the Japanese and developed to become today's well-known tempura.

At the restaurant, we ordered shrimp, squid, eel, and the original green beans tempura. The tempura was served on rice with a side of miso soup. We also ordered Kirin beer, since beer always goes well with fried food.

As of 2015, five major companies dominate the beer market in Japan, with a combined sale of above 2.5 million kiloliters per year. These companies include Asahi Group Holdings Ltd., Kirin Holdings Co. Ltd., Suntory Holdings Ltd., Sapporo Holdings Ltd., and Orion Breweries Ltd.[28] However, beer is only one of the alcoholic drinks produced in

Japan. The Japanese liquor market is actually one of the biggest liquor markets in the world, and it also includes whiskey, and the national beverage: sake.

Japanese whiskey first became commercially available in 1924, produced by Torii at Yamazaki distillery[29]. Torii was a pharmaceutical wholesaler who imported western liquor. After a few years in the alcohol industry, Torii decided to make a Japanese whiskey for Japanese people. For that goal, he built the first Japanese distillery, Yamazaki, in Kyoto. Today, the most widely available blended, single malt whiskeys, and blended malt whiskeys are produced by *Suntory* and *Nikka* distilleries.

Good to know: Japanese whiskey is so good that in 2014, the Yamazaki Single Malt Sherry Cask 2013 won the world's best whiskey title[30].

Sake, the national beverage, dates back to the Nara period (710−794). It is made from fermented rice, water, koji mold, and yeast[31]. The brewing process for sake is similar to beer brewing, but with minor differences. While the conversion from starch to sugar, and from sugar to alcohol occurs in two distinct steps for beer brewing, in sake brewing, they occur simultaneously[32]. Another difference between the two is that Sake has a higher alcohol content than beer (18%-20% versus 3%-9%). Sake is often warmed in a porcelain bottle called *tokkuri* and served in a small porcelain cup called *sakazuki*.

Sake can be served warm or cold. Traditionally, it used to only be served warm, but brewing advances produced a new type of sake[33]. The new sake has different flavor profiles that can be destroyed by warming it. Most of the premium sake available today is best served slightly chilled, since cooling it too much masks some of its flavors.

Sources:

[1] https://en.wikipedia.org/wiki/Bento

[2] http://www.seriouseats.com/2014/06/guide-japanese-pickles-tsukemono.html

[3] http://jpninfo.com/27841

[4] http://www.japan-talk.com/jt/new/miso-soup

[5] https://okinawa.stripes.com/news/japan-best-foods-life-are-fermented

[6] http://kyoto.travel/en/traveller_kit/tools_smoking

[7] http://www.jreast.co.jp/e/pass/suica.html?src=gnavi#category05

[8] https://matcha-jp.com/en/836

[9] http://weburbanist.com/2010/06/06/narrower-towers-20-of-japans-thinnest-buildings/

[10] http://www.nihonsun.com/2009/06/17/precarious-parking-options-in-japan/

[11] https://en.wikipedia.org/wiki/Kawaii

[12] https://en.wikipedia.org/wiki/Tokyo_Skytree

[13] http://bestlivingjapan.com/kameido-tenjin-shrine/

[14] http://www.japan-guide.com/e/e2057.html

[15] http://www.ancient.eu/Fujiwara_Clan/

[16] https://koto-guide.blogspot.ca/2015/01/kameido-tenjin.html

[17] https://www.jnto.org.au/about-jnto/

[18] http://jpninfo.com/25747

[19] https://tokyocheapo.com/entertainment/sensoji-temple-guide/

[20] http://www.japan-guide.com/e/e3001.html

[21]https://www.tripadvisor.ca/ShowUserReviews-g1066461-d320447-r203914460-Senso_ji_Temple-Taito_Tokyo_Tokyo_Prefecture_Kanto.html

[22] http://www.japan-guide.com/e/e2057.html

[23] http://blog.hinomaple.com/2010/02/09/temples-of-tokyo-part-i-sensoji/

[24] http://blog.hinomaple.com/2010/02/09/temples-of-tokyo-

part-i-sensoji/

[25] https://www.japan-guide.com/e/e629.html

[26] http://www.japan-talk.com/jt/new/oden

[27] http://www.bbc.com/travel/story/20170808-the-truth-about-japanese-tempura

[28] https://blogs.wsj.com/briefly/2016/08/31/japans-beer-industry-the-numbers/

[29] https://en.wikipedia.org/wiki/Japanese_whisky

[30]https://www.washingtonpost.com/news/morning-mix/wp/2014/11/05/japan-beats-scotland-to-win-worlds-best-whiskey-title/?noredirect=on&utm_term=.6a2d97956154

[31] http://www.japan-guide.com/e/e2037_sake.html

[32] https://en.wikipedia.org/wiki/Sake

[33] http://www.esake.com/Sake-Food/Etiquette/etiquette.html

3

Day 3: Ueno Park, Conveyor Belt Sushi, View of Tokyo, and Exploring Small Alleys

To save time, we started the day in the hotel Sunny restaurant again. Only this time, we ordered different things. My husband ordered a bento box like the day before, but with chicken instead of fish. I ordered two panini sandwiches, one with tuna salad, and the other with ham and cheese. I like eating panini for breakfast, but usually, on vacation, I enjoy ordering new things. I am so glad I didn't this time. The paninis were delicious! The cheese, ham, and tuna salad had a very different flavor from the western style I am accustomed to. Without asking, I could see my husband was also very content with his breakfast. I knew it because his plate was empty, and he usually doesn't eat anything for breakfast. With good value for the price, we ended up paying ¥1,400 for both breakfasts.

After breakfast, we took the subway to Ueno-onshi-koen Park, commonly called Ueno Park. This park used to be part of Kaneiji temple and also serves as a cherry blossom viewing destination[1]. In 1873, after the Boshin Civil War, the park was rebuilt to be the first public western style park in Japan[2]. Later, it became a center of arts, culture, and education. Today, the park surrounds a zoo, the Tokyo University of Arts, and several museums (including the Tokyo National Museum, the National Museum for Western Art, the Tokyo Metropolitan Art Museum, and the National Science Museum).

When you walk in this park, it is very clear that it is indeed an arts center. During our short walk in the park, we came across a singer, a multi-instrumentalist, and a group of dancers. The park has a very relaxing atmosphere. It combines nature, religion, and arts into one green lung.

Good to know: It is usually considered rude to eat on the streets in Japan, whereas it is acceptable to eat while sitting on a public bench. However, finding a public bench may turn out as a challenge since public benches are not too common in Japan.

Sites from Ueno park. On the right: a multi-instrumentalist.

We left the park shortly after we arrived because it was a very sunny day. Although the park is very pleasant, it doesn't offer many shaded areas. After leaving the park, we headed to Ameya yokocho, or Ameyoko. Ameyoko is a street market with a large variety of clothing shops, seafood shops, some restaurants, and food vendors. There, we bought a ¥200 warm fish-shaped pastry filled with red beans, called *Taiyaki*.

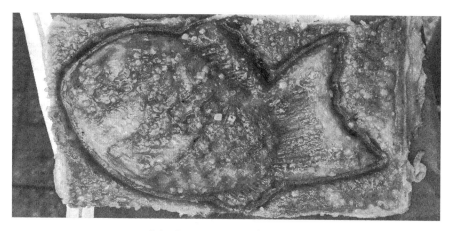

Fish shaped pastry (Taiyaki).

Later, we found a cute little shop that offers animal-shaped keychains made from leather. After we picked a panda keychain for our niece, the salesman asked if we wanted to write a dedication on it. We said yes, and he gave us a piece of paper on which we wrote our niece's name. I handed the salesman the note and he took it to the back of the store. When he returned with the keychain, I noticed her name was written on it in my handwriting! It made the gift so much more personal, and frankly, very cool.

Walking down the street, we noticed a game center with many claw machines (or crane machines), arcades, and photo booths. Photo booths in Japan, or *Purikura*, became very popular in the last 20 years[3]. The reason for this is that they offer much more than just a printed photograph. When Purikura first became popular, it used to frame the picture with popular Japanese characters (e.g., Hello kitty). Since then, it has evolved to offer users the ability to add makeup, enlarge their eyes, or add stickers and text to the photos. In the game center, we had our photos taken by a "Rumor" Purikura.

The way a Purikura works is first you pay, and then you simply follow the pose instructions on the screen. Then, you go around the machine to a screen showing your just-taken photos. There, you can add stickers, makeup, or writings on the photos, while a timer counts down on the corner of the screen. Lastly, you go to the other side of the machine, where you'll find another screen. This screen provides you with the option to enter your email address so you can get a digital copy of the photos. You can also simply print the photos without providing your email address. You can print two copies for ¥400. This is such a ridiculous experience, and yet, very fun.

Left: Sushi-shaped keychains in a claw machine. Right: arcade.

All the fun and games made us hungry for some sushi. We went to a conveyor belt sushi restaurant called *Oedo Kaitenzushi*. The restaurant was busy, so we had to wait for a few minutes until we were seated. The restaurant had three chefs making nigiri sushi, with a conveyor belt around them. Between every two seats around the conveyor belt, was a faucet with hot water, green tea powder, and a ginger jar. The chefs were working non-stop, creating beautiful nigiri with a small amount of wasabi in between the rice and the topping.

Each time the chefs finished making one type of sushi, they put a bundle of plates on the conveyor belt. Each bundle of plates containing the same sushi type had a plate with a sign going in front of it. A diner can simply reach his hand and grab the plate as it passes in front of him. For those not patient enough, there was also an option to ask the chefs directly for a desired sushi from the menu. When a person is finished, the waiter simply counts his plates. Since the price of each plate is ¥150, the waiter multiplies the number of the plates by ¥150 to get the total price of the meal.

We ended up with 28 empty plates for the both of us, at the sum of ¥4,200. We tried a few interesting things like raw shrimp nigiri, raw baby squid sushi, sea urchin, and crab salad sushi. Honestly, it was not the sushi I came to Japan for. Don't get me wrong, it was still better than most places I know, but it didn't have the WOW factor. It is a good solution for people in a hurry or people who want to try different kinds of sushi quickly.

Good to know: Different conveyor belt sushi restaurants have a different method to set the price. Some have the same price for each plate, while others have a different price for different plate colors.

Good to know: Ginger is used for cleansing the palate between different types of sushi. It is considered very rude to eat sushi and a piece of ginger with it. The wasabi is used to enhance the flavor of the fish and to kill any parasites the fish may have.

Good to know: Nigiri sushi already has wasabi in between the fish and the rice, so there is no need to add it yourself[4].

Tip: Dip a nigiri in soy sauce fish side-down so the rice won't fall apart.

Left: Tobikko (Flying Fish Roe) sushi. Center: sushi on a conveyor belt. Right: raw baby squid sushi at Oedo Kaitenzushi restaurant.

Conveyor belt sushi, *Kaiten-zushi*, was invented in 1958 in Osaka, by a restaurant owner named Yoshiaki Shiraishi[5]. After visiting the Asahi beer factory, Yoshiaki was inspired to incorporate a conveyor belt at his restaurant. He did this to increase the number of customers in his restaurant while keeping the same amount of staff, and low prices. The conveyor belt sushi had a large increase in popularity following its feature in the Osaka World Expo in 1970. During the 80s, eating out became popular, and by the 90s, cheap restaurants gained a big interest. It was at this time the conveyor belts gained widespread popularity[6].

The conveyor belt sushi is certainly good for one thing: to fill you up completely. Outside of the restaurant I noticed an ad accurately describing the way I felt:

Ad next to Oedo Kaitenzushi restaurant.

From the restaurant, we went to the subway. We took the subway towards *Higashi Shinjuku* and six minutes away from the station, we passed by a café with a very cute dessert collection. The name of the café is Squall café and it's a chain in Japan. It's located right below a karaoke place. I went for the coffee, but my husband and friends actually had room left for dessert. They ordered the signature toast filled with ice cream, fruits, and whipped cream. Amazingly, this dessert is made from an ENTIRE loaf of bread. They said they loved it, but I could tell by my husband's facial expression that it was too much for him, especially after the sushi experience.

Left: bread-shaped stuffed toys. Right: window display at Squall cafe.

One of the things we didn't have a chance to try during this trip is karaoke. Karaoke is an interactive entertainment form that originated in Japan. During a karaoke, music is being played, while a person sings the synchronized lyrics that appear on a screen[7]. Although the karaoke machine was invented in the 1970s[8], it is still a very popular form of entertainment enjoyed by all ages in Japan.

Good to know: There are different kinds of karaoke: a private box, where you have a small room to yourself, or karaoke bars, where people sing in front of everyone present. For more guidance on what to expect, visit: *japan-guid.com.*

After the coffee/dessert, we slowly dragged ourselves to *Isetan Kaikan*. Isetan Kaikan is a shopping mall located close to the Squall café. We didn't go to the mall for the houseware or fashion stores, we went to look at food. Many of the department stores in Japan (or *depato*) have a food floor. The food floor is usually located in the basement and is called *depachika*. Unlike the food court in western countries, depachika isn't fast food oriented. It actually looks very much like a department store floor. Different counters sell beautifully made and packed food items. The variety in food items is amazing, and it is difficult to focus only on one thing. Like the variety of food items, the prices are very different from counter to counter. You may find a bento box for ¥1,780, a box with a single muskmelon for ¥16,200, or a box of cherries for ¥8,640.

The reason for the seemingly outrageous fruit prices in Japan is that they are not considered just fruits, but more like edible art. Fruits in Japan are offered to gods at altars and therefore are a symbol of respect[9]. Many people give fruits as a gift to people they feel grateful to during the *chugen* and *seibo* holidays. Giving gifts in Japan is not done only during holidays or birthdays; it is a big part of the culture. People tend to bring gifts when visiting friends and family as a way to return a favor, or just because they want to do something nice for someone[10]. Giving perishable gifts in Japan is preferable because of the small living spaces most Japanese have. This status of fruits as gifts made a market for high-end fruit shops in Japan. One known shop is called *Sembikiya*. Sembikiya is thought to be responsible for the luxury fruit obsession in Japan because it was the pioneer in its field[11].

Tip: If you are looking for cheap eats, the food floor of the department store *Isetan Kaikan* isn't the best place for you as it is more on the pricey side. Instead, try going to the more affordable *Tokyu*, located in Shibuya.

Good to know: You are not allowed to eat in the *depachika* (food floor of a department store). Usually, there is a designated eating area. Another option is to take your food to go.

The variety in food items in the food floor at Isetan Kaikan.

After leaving the *Isetan Kaikan*, we hopped on a subway and went to the Metropolitan Government Building. This building was the tallest building in Tokyo up to 2007[12]. We went to this building because it is one of the only places in Tokyo that offer a view of Tokyo for free. Tourists are allowed to access the 360-degree observatory located on the 45th floor, along with cafés and gift shops. However, before being allowed to enter the building, there are many security measures to go through. The reason for the elaborated security is that the government building is home to the assembly hall of the metropolitan government of Tokyo.

We arrived at the building grounds before sunset and saw a long line of people waiting to get in. After the line progressed a bit, we noticed a one-hour approximation wait sign. We couldn't see the actual length of the line from where we stood because it was hidden around the corner of the building. While my husband and friends saved me a spot in line, I went to explore the actual line length. It seemed pretty long, but it was constantly moving, so we decided to wait it out. After exactly 24 minutes, we entered the building. First, we passed through security, and then we were jammed like sardines in an elevator. We reached the 45th floor right at the end of the sunset, and the view was amazing. After a few more minutes, it became pitch dark and the view changed to a sea of lights. This view was definitely worth the wait.

Tip: Try timing your arrival so you would enter the Metropolitan government building right before the sunset begins. This way, you can enjoy the view of Tokyo and enjoy the romantic atmosphere when the night covers the city.

Left: Tokyo government building. Right: view from the 45th floor of the government building.

After we finished taking pictures from every possible angle, we headed towards *Golden Gai*. Golden Gai is a nightlife street with many small bars. I was really excited about Golden Gai because the articles I read before coming to Japan praised it. I read sentences like, "only in Golden Gai can you see vestiges of the Japanese capital's postwar nightlife – down to earth, locally-minded and still wonderfully bizarre[13]," and it made me so impatient for my visit. Golden Gai is definitely not "down to earth" or "locally-minded," but it does have a lot of history. It is one of the few old-fashioned Tokyo places that survived the earthquake in 1923, the air bombing during WWII, and the redevelopment that followed the war. After the war, Tokyo was rebuilt, and many small buildings and neighborhoods were exchanged for high rises[14]. Nowadays, Golden Gai consists of six small alleys with approximately two hundred tiny bars surrounded by post-war high-rise buildings.

When we arrived at Golden Gai, I was a bit disappointed because almost all the people I saw were loud tourists. It took us a while to choose a bar, or more accurately, to find a bar with four free spots and fewer tourists. The bar we entered could only fit seven people, which is not uncommon in Golden Gai. When we entered the bar, a Japanese couple sitting at the bar and the bartender greeted us. We ordered sake and whiskey, but instead, we got flavored ice. The glasses we got were completely filled with ice and had a few drops of alcohol poured on top. There was so little alcohol that the ice didn't even melt.

Usually, people go to bars in Japan so they can drink and talk with friends and strangers. However, the Japanese couple sitting next to us hardly spoke English and as a result, the conversation between us didn't flow naturally and was very awkward. The bartender probably didn't understand English that well either, or simply wasn't interested in conversing with us. Bottom line, ¥1,000 for a drink that mostly consists of ice seems a bit much. The overall experience was depressing. You can find much better establishments elsewhere; establishments that offer food and real drinks.

Good to know: Seeing that most establishments in Golden Gai are very small, they commonly have a table charge (Tsukidashi).

Good to know: Opening hours for most bars in Golden Gai are 5:30PM Mon-Sat, and 8PM on Sunday.

Three minutes away from the Golden Gai, we saw a cute café that had a white rabbit painted on the wall and guard statues made out of playing cards. You may have guessed it: it's an Alice in Wonderland inspired café. This café is called Alice in Fantasy Book, and it is a themed café. Japan has various themed cafés with themes including cute, like Alice in Fantasy Book; bizarre, like a prison-themed restaurant; scary, like an asylum-themed restaurant or vampire-themed restaurant; and fun, like a fishing restaurant[15]. Whatever restaurant you choose, it will be a unique experience. In Alice in Fantasy Book, each person has to order a food and drink item and pay ¥500 to enter. The walls, tables, menu, and even bathrooms are decorated according to the Alice in Wonderland theme. Even the waitresses are dressed like Alice and

42

are named Alice. To get their attention, all you have to do is simply call out "Alice." Unlike everything else, the music in the restaurant wasn't strictly related to Alice in Wonderland. It was a collection of songs from all Disney movies and it was in English.

We ordered drinks that were very colorful and sweet, and foie gras that was very pleasant. We ended up paying a total of ¥3,950 per couple. The experience was a little tacky, but I still enjoyed it. My husband, on the other hand, was very unhappy. When I told him it feels like being in a dream, he said, "A nightmare is also a kind of a dream."

Left: Golden Gai. Center: sweet Tsukidashi at Alice in Fantasy Book cafe. Right: The cafe's menu.

After dining with Alice, we headed towards *Omoide Yokocho* in the Shinjuku West gate area. This area used to be known for its street vendors and the black market, but it has since been rebuilt (in 1946, after the WWII), and now it consists of more than 70 street stalls and restaurants[16]. *Omoide Yokocho* is also known as memory lane, but it is also referred to as Yakitori Alley. It got its name because it is a popular spot to enjoy Yakitori and Japanese liquor, while absorbing the history of the city.

In memory lane, we went to *Kappetei* Izakaya. We were seated on the second floor, next to a window with a view of the train. We ordered different kinds of Yakitori for ¥2,500 per couple. Our favorite was chicken thighs with leek and the least favorite was chicken intestine. We also got a small complementary noodle and shrimp salad. Overall, it wasn't the best Yakitori place we visited up to that point, but definitely the best noodle and shrimp salad place. Either way, this is where our day came to an end.

Good to know: Try going to the Yakitori alley in the evening after 4PM, when most Yakitori spots open.

Left: noodle and shrimp salad. Right: Yakitori at Kappetei Izakaya.

Sources:

[1]   https://www.jnto.go.jp/eng/spot/gardens/uenoonshikoen-park.html

[2] http://www.japan-guide.com/e/e3019.html

[3]   https://en.japantravel.com/tokyo/the-amazing-purikura-machines/5054

[4]   https://blog.opentable.com/2017/sushi-etiquette-dos-and-donts-from-6-top-sushi-chefs-hackdining/

[5] https://www.seattlefish.com/2015/03/11/food-move-history-conveyor-belt-sushi/

[6] https://en.wikipedia.org/wiki/Conveyor_belt_sushi

[7] http://www.japan-guide.com/e/e2066.html

[8] https://en.wikipedia.org/wiki/Karaoke

[9] http://www.cnn.com/travel/article/japan-luxury-expensive-fruit/index.html

[10] http://zine375.eserver.org/zine1.html

[11]http://www.slate.com/articles/news_and_politics/roads/2017/03/japan_s_high_end_fruit_market_elevates_produce_to_works_of_art.html

[12] http://www.japan-guide.com/e/e3011_tocho.html

[13] https://www.roughguides.com/article/tokyos-tiniest-drinking-dens-a-guide-to-golden-gai/

[14] http://www.unmissabletokyo.com/golden-gai

[15] http://booky-wordpress-staging.us-east-1.elasticbeanstalk.com/blog/unique-japan-cafes/

[16]https://en.japantravel.com/tokyo/shinjuku-s-memory-lane-%E6%80%9D%E3%81%84%E5%87%BA%E6%A8%AA%E4%B8%81/5025

4

Day 4: Fish Market, Tea House, Ramen Street, Shibuya Crossing, and Cat Café

Today we had plans for breakfast and they didn't involve the area next to our hotel. We took the subway to Tsukiji station. When we exited the station, we noticed a Buddhist temple called *Tsukiji Hongwanji* and we decided to take a detour from our breakfast destination and go in. This temple is just a branch of the *Nishi Hongwanji*. The mother temple of Nishi Hongwanji is actually located in Kyoto. The Tsukiji Hongwanji temple was rebuilt after the Great Fire of 1657 destroyed the previous temple. However, the replacement temple wasn't rebuilt on the original site, but on land reclaimed from the sea. This temple was later called Tsukiji, literally meaning "built-up land[1]." The Tsukiji temple was also destroyed during the Great Kanto earthquake in 1923 and the temple we see today dates back to 1934 when the reconstruction was completed. The inside of the temple contains an altar for Amida Buddha, a shrine of prince Shotoku, scrolls of the seven pure land patriarchs, an altar for Shinran Shonin, and a scroll of the mother temple in Kyoto. When we entered the temple, we were greeted and welcomed to enter. We were told we could take pictures and ask questions about the temple.

The Tsukiji Hongwanji Temple.

The temple was a detour on our way to Tsukiji market. While fruits, vegetables, and flowers are sold in Tsukiji market, it is mainly famous for being a fish market. The fish market handles over 2,000 tons of seafood products per day. It also hosts a daily tuna auction for businesses in Tokyo[2].

Good to know: Each day, only 120 people are allowed to visit the tuna auction in Tsukiji market on a first come- first serve manner. Visitors usually start waiting in line for the Osakana Fukyu Center (Fish Information Center) at the *Kachidoki* Gate a few hours before 5AM. For more information on how to plan a visit to the tuna auction, visit tokyocheapo.com.

My parents visited Japan a few years back and they told me about the auction. They said it was exciting to watch people bid for the enormous fish, but mostly, they didn't fully understand what was going on. Everything was done very quickly and in Japanese. This made it difficult for my parents to follow and they were a little bored. After we heard their stories, we decided to skip the auction. Instead, we chose to check out the tuna in a different way. A few sushi restaurants surround the Tsukiji market and these restaurants conveniently get their fish supplies (as well as the auctioned Tuna) from the market.

During our preparation for the Tsukiji market trip, we found *Sushi Tomi* restaurant online. Sushi Tomi had a great rating online (4 out of 5) and very convenient operating hours (7AM-11:30PM). When we arrived at the restaurant, it was already full. We asked for a table for four people and went outside to wait to be seated. Outside, we saw another sushi restaurant neighboring Sushi Tomi. In front of the restaurant, we saw a sign with a long list of menu items and next to the sign, we saw a large tuna fish head on an ice tray. This is a genius way to advertise the restaurant. The restaurant puts the fish head on display to attract clients that pass by, by showing them how fresh their fish is. The fact that even on this warm day, the fish didn't have any smell and it glistened in the sun almost attracted us away from Sushi Tomi. Nonetheless, we stayed faithful to our original choice.

A sushi restaurant near Tsukiji market.

After 10 minutes of excited wait, we were called to enter. We were seated at the bar- a perfect location that allowed us to observe the chefs while they prepared the sushi. To become a sushi chef in Japan, aka *itamae*, a person usually has to train for 5 years as an apprentice. During this time, the apprentice perfects the preparation of rice by following a strict recipe every day. Only when the senior itamae is satisfied with the rice, can the apprentice be promoted[3]. After the promotion, the apprentice becomes *wakiita*. The wakiita is in charge of cutting fish and preparing the sides that come with the sushi (e.g., grating the wasabi). During this role, the wakiita learns how to interact with the customers. Later, the wakiita might be allowed to prepare sushi for take-out orders. Only after perfecting the wakiita role, can a person become an itamae.

As I said before, the restaurant was very full, so it took some time to prepare our orders. Meanwhile, we looked at the decoration of the restaurant, enjoyed a warm green tea, and watched the chefs while they worked. The precise hand movements of the chefs are mesmerizing. It is unbelievable to think it took them years of practice to get to this ranking.

We ordered a *Chirashizushi*, which is a bowl of rice topped with a variety of sashimi. The Chirashizushi we ordered had different cuts of tuna sashimi served on rice for a total of ¥4,500 per couple. The dishes we were served were a piece of perfection. The fish was cut into big, identical pieces, and each piece had its own role on the plate. Accompanying and accenting the main actors were freshly ground wasabi, ginger, radish, seaweed, and pickled cabbage. The way they were assembled created a vivid feast for the eyes. Since people first eat with their eyes, my appetite increased dramatically when I first saw the bowl.

We started off with the least fatty piece of tuna and worked our way up the fatty ladder. While taking the first bite, my eyes began to water.

It was incredibly tasty. I couldn't believe it was the "worst" of the cuts. My husband and I ate in silence, not to take attention away from our meal. Climbing the fatty ladder just increased my excitement and enjoyment from the meal. When we dug our way to the rice, we were already mostly full. Knowing that we had a full day of food opportunities before us, we didn't want to fill up on a simple bowl of rice, but after taking the first bite of rice, we couldn't stop ourselves. It was just sour enough, just sweet enough, and with the perfect amount of soy sauce. The grains were held together, but also separate. It was without a doubt the best rice I've ever eaten.

My husband was a bit disappointed he didn't order nigiri instead of the bowl, which would have allowed him to enjoy the combination of fish and rice simultaneously. After finishing this incredible meal, we could finally appreciate the amount of effort that goes into becoming a sushi chef.

Good to know: Many sushi chefs in Japan agree that the rice is the most important part of the sushi[4]. For this reason, my husband always prefers ordering nigiri instead of sashimi. This way, he enjoys the perfect harmony between the rice and the fish.

Originally, the first version of sushi (*Narezushi*) was a piece of fish preserved in fermented rice. The rice was thrown away, while only the fish was consumed[5]. The Narezushi originated in China and arrived in Japan during the 8th century. The first-time raw fish was consumed with vinegared rice was during the 1800s, in a dish called *Nigirizushi* (made of a piece of raw fish on a rice ball).

Two Chirashizushi bowls at Sushi Tomi Restaurant.

When we finished eating, we wanted to thank the chefs for the brilliant sushi, but unfortunately, they didn't speak English. I used Google Translate to translate "amazing" into Japanese. Hoping the translation was correct, I showed the chefs the translation on my phone, and said: "arigato gozaimasu" (thank you). They smiled humbly and replied with "arigato gozaimasu." The experience was indeed superb, and a flawless way to start the day.

After breakfast, we looked around the houseware stores located in the Tsukiji market. Due to the high prices and the massive amount of people around, we decided to cut the market tour short.

Good to know: Tsukiji market is planned to move to Toyosu to make room for the Tokyo 2020 Olympics[6]. The move is scheduled for Sep-Oct 2018[7].

It was a warm sunny day, suitable for a stroll in the park. We headed to Hamarikyu gardens, located 15 minutes away from Tsukiji market. The Hamarikyu gardens were built during the Edo period and were kept private until they were eventually opened to the public[8]. Although the gardens are public, they aren't free. The entry to the gardens costs ¥300. They are surrounded by tall skyscrapers, and they provide a place to de-stress and enjoy some nature in the middle of the city.

51

Some of the things you may find in the garden are saltwater ponds, a tea house, and a historical duck hunting ground. The gardens have many unshaded areas and are very well kept.

After a stroll in the gardens, we decided to visit the tea house located in the bay of one of the ponds. The tea house also provides a serene view of the pond and gardens. Moreover, the tea house provides you with a fresh matcha tea and a small dessert for ¥600. The bitter matcha is accented by the sweet bean-filled dessert and offers an uplifting experience.

It was the first time in my life I tasted matcha tea. I expected it to be more like green tea because it's made from ground green tea leaves. However, the flavor and texture were entirely different. The matcha tea has significantly more caffeine than regular green tea, so its taste is more bitter. Additionally, to prepare a proper matcha tea, it has to be stirred with a whisk to form a thick foam. The foam gives a very airy texture to the matcha and enhances its flavor. Luckily for me, I enjoy bitter airy drinks, so I loved it.

Left: the tea house at Hamarikyu gardens. Right: match tea and sweet bean-filled desserts.

Tea ceremonies in Japan originated in the 9th century when tea houses were built for a medicinal purpose[9]. Tea was used as a medicine for the mind, body, and spirit. Later, tea ceremonies became a sort of entertainment for the upper class. During the 15th century, a tea master named Shukō envisioned tea as a way to remove stress and find enlightenment in everyday life. His idea is present in today's tea houses, where simplicity plays a vital role. Tea houses are commonly simple, wooden structures located in the gardens of private homes and on the grounds of temples, museums, and parks[10].

Good to know: You are not allowed to enter a tea house with your outdoor shoes. If there is an outside deck, you will be provided with slippers to only be worn there.

Energized from the matcha tea, we took the train to Tokyo station. Right outside the station, there are stairs to a basement with a cluster of 8 Ramen restaurants, called *Ramen Street*. Each one of the restaurants had a line, but the longest one by far was for *Rokurinsha*. Rokurinsha restaurant was featured by chef David Chang in a TV show called *The Mind of a Chef*. While Rokurinsha restaurant is undoubtedly fantastic, it's believed that all restaurants on Ramen Street are the best Ramen restaurants in Japan[11]. After a short walk down Ramen Street, we stood in line for the restaurant opposite to *Rokurinsha*. We chose this place on the following premises: first, we believed any of the restaurants in the Ramen Street are good, and second, there were mostly locals inside and usually it means that it's not a tourist-oriented restaurant. The line wasn't long, and after 10-15 minutes we reached the vending machine where you order your meal.

Vending machines are very common in Japan. In fact, there are over 5 million vending machines throughout the nation[12]. The large quantity of vending machines and a huge variety in their content (mostly food, hot, and cold beverages, but sometimes umbrellas, socks, etc.) reveal a story of the Japanese people. There are two well-known facts about Japanese people: they have long-hours work days[13] and there's a nation-wide fascination with automation[14]. A vending machine combines these two features to provide a convenient solution for the hard-working person.

The vending machine at the entrance to the restaurant had pictures of the Ramen menu on it (thankfully), and some buttons in Japanese that allow you to add toppings to the Ramen. We chose one entrée as is (noodles in broth with a few toppings), and one with extra meat. After paying a total of ¥1,930 for 2 Ramens, the vending machine issued a ticket with our order, which the hostess took after she showed us to our table. About five minutes later, we had an exact replica of the Ramen displayed in the vending machine. It looked like they took a picture of the Ramen just before serving it to us. We asked for some garlic on the side, because we love the added flavor. The Ramen was absolutely fabulous. It was meaty, comforting, and most importantly, umami. We enjoy Ramen at home, and I actually experimented and perfected a recipe I make every week. I regret to say that after eating this Ramen, I realized my own recipe was a sad imitation.

Tip: The polite way to eat Ramen is while slurping the noodles because this way you convey how delicious it is, while also cooling the noodles[15]. Moreover, the flavors of the Ramen are enhanced when slurping[16]. So, when in Japan, act like a Japanese and slurp away.

Tip: If you want to avoid standing in line for one of the restaurants in Ramen Street, try to arrive after lunch hours (lunch is between 11:30AM-2:00PM) and before dinner hours (starting at 6PM). When we finished eating it was 4PM, on a Saturday during the Golden Week. By that time, the only restaurant with a line was Rokurinsha.

Ramen in the Ramen street.

After we finished enjoying the best Ramen I've ever had, we took the subway to Shibuya. Shibuya is a district in Tokyo that became very popular among young people during the 1980s due to its fashion department stores. In the 1990s it also became a center for the IT industry[17]. Nowadays, except for the vast variety of department stores and businesses in Shibuya, it is also well known for two more reasons. First, it is home to the busiest intersection in Japan, and perhaps in the world. This intersection is called Shibuya crossing. The unique thing about Shibuya crossing is that each time the traffic stops, it stops all around the junction, and there is a flow of people crossing the intersection in every direction. This buzzing of people somewhat resembles a beehive, where the density is high and the movements are quick and precise. Due to this high density, the intersection has been targeted by advertising companies that display ads on the large screens overlooking it. The film industry also targets this crossing, and it was featured in "Lost in Translation," "The Fast and the Furious: Tokyo Drift," and more[18].

The second thing Shibuya crossing is known for is the statue of a dog named *Hachiko*. In 1924, Eizaburo Ueno, a professor at Tokyo University, adopted a purebred Akita dog named Hachiko. A true companionship bloomed between the professor and the dog, and they spent every possible moment together. When the professor had to go to work, Hachiko would accompany him to the train station in Shibuya. Hachiko would return to the station at the end of the day to meet his owner as he returns home. One day, in 1925, the professor passed away while at work and didn't show up when Hachiko waited for him at the station. After the professor's passing, Hachiko was adopted by his relatives, but Hachiko kept making the same dual daily trip to the station in the hopes of seeing his master. He kept doing so each day, until the day he died. On March 8, 1935, his body was found next to Shibuya station. Due to the dog's incredible loyalty, Hachiko became a symbol of faithfulness. Now, a bronze statue of Hachiko is displayed next to Shibuya station. A few meters away from the statue, on the station wall, there is also a mosaic of Hachiko[19].

Hachiko's story was an inspiration for a movie that hit the screens in 2009, called "Hachi: A Dog's Tale." In the movie, the character of the professor is played by Richard Gere.

Left: Shibuya crossing. Right: a bronze statue of Hachiko.

Walking in Shibuya, or even standing on the sidewalk and looking at people, is a noteworthy and overwhelming experience. It is totally captivating, like watching water flow or fire burn.

Tip: Right next to Shibuya intersection there is a Starbucks branch located on the second floor. This Starbucks provides a very pretty elevated view of Shibuya Crossing, but it is VERY busy as well[20].

While visiting the Hachiko statue, we noticed there was a sleeping cat at the dog's feet. It seemed like the cat was trying to steal the attention away from the dog. My husband and I joked that the cat probably comes to the statue daily, and once it dies, there will be a statue of it there as well. Jokes aside, Japanese people take their pets very seriously. Dressed up dogs pushed down the street in a stroller were not an uncommon sight during our time in Japan. Places such as dog spas, designer pet clothing shops, and restaurants where a pet can eat at the table with its human family have gained a lot of popularity in the past 10 years[21]. Animal cafés are also trendy in Japan. You may find a cat, bunny, owl, bird, or even snake cafés in Tokyo alone[22].

After passing the Shibuya crossing a few times, we decided to go to a cat café. We went there because we were very intrigued by the concept. We went to *Cat Café MoCHA*, located just a five minute walk from Shibuya station. It costs ¥200 every 10 minutes, and a beverage costs ¥350. Before you enter, you get shoe covers and need to apply a hand sanitizer to clean your hands. During your visit, you can play and pet the cats, but you are not allowed to pick them up. You can also buy treats and feed them.

I was a bit disappointed with my visit to the cat café. The cats were cute, I'll admit, but they were too calm and bored – probably a result of the constant attention – so they were unreactive when petted. Most of the cats were sleeping and didn't even flinch when touched. After trying to make friends with almost every cat in the café, finally, I found a Russian blue relaxing near the stairs. I bonded with it a little, or at least I felt like I did because it was the only cat that purred while I petted it. We stayed there for about 30 minutes – more than enough in my opinion.

After spending some time with Japanese cats, we decided to split up into 2 groups. Our friends wanted to do some shopping in the numerous stores around Shibuya, and we wanted to continue to the next destination in our plan: *Tokyu food show*. Tokyu is a department store near Shibuya station, and in its basement there is a food hall considered one of the largest and most diversified in Tokyo[23]. In contrast to the food hall at *Isetan Kaikan*, Tokyu's food hall is much more affordable and down to earth. Although the prices are lower, this doesn't affect the quality of the food. Here you can find food stalls associated with popular restaurants around Tokyo.

There is a large variety of foods you may find in the Tokyu food show: Chinese, Vietnamese, Indian, and French dishes are just an example of the diversification present. As in most department food halls, the food is mostly take-out (or take-away) and is not supposed to be eaten on the premises. Mostly, we just walked around watching the workers craft beautiful handmade food. At one of the food stands we got a yummy deep-fried potato pastry for ¥160, and we quickly went outside to eat it. After reaching the point of no return – the heart of the pastry – we realized it was filled with melted cheese. Frankly, who would even want to stop at this point?

A few of the food options in the Tokyu food show.

While my husband and I waited to meet up with our friends, we walked around the Shibuya station area and accidentally noticed the *Ichiran Ramen* restaurant. Ichiran Ramen was first established in the early 1960s. Today, it is a very well-liked chain in Japan and around the world. Some people even claim it's the best Ramen in the world[24], while the place we visited in Ramen Street still stays first place in my heart. The unusual thing you can find in this restaurant is the dining experience. Unlike most restaurants, Ichiran Ramen allows you to detach from the crowd, and eat in peace without any distraction.

After standing in line to enter the restaurant (most likely there will be a line), you will be given a sheet of paper to fill out your preferences of Ramen. From our experience, we would stick to the recommended Ramen, since it is recommended for a reason. Next, you will be seated at a counter with partitions between seats. The partitions may be opened if you wish, but you can leave them as is for some privacy. In front of you, you can see the middle portion of the waiters running around fulfilling orders. Once the waiter gives you your order, he will bow down 90 degrees (so you can see his head), and then close the partition in front of you. Now, finally, you can feel entirely at peace, and enjoy your Ramen on your own.

We liked the Ramen in Ichiran, but after the excellent ramen we had for lunch, it was a bit of a letdown. Still good enough but not great. Yet, far better than most. Probably we would have liked it better if we hadn't had Ramen several hours earlier. We ended up paying ¥890 per person.

Ramen in Ichiran Ramen restaurant.

At the end of the day, we took our luggage from Lungwood hotel and moved to Mystays hotel. It is only a two minute walk from Lungwood hotel, and it offered a lower price per room (about ¥9,500 per night).

Sources

[1] Information taken from the pamphlet at Tsukiji Hongwanji

[2] http://www.japan-guide.com/e/e3021.html

[3] https://en.wikipedia.org/wiki/Itamae

[4] https://lifehacker.com/the-essential-keys-to-making-perfect-sushi-rice-1793199724

[5] http://www.eat-japan.com/sushi-perfect/sushi-knwoledge/sushi-history/

[6] https://www.theguardian.com/world/2017/jun/20/worlds-largest-fish-market-will-finally-move-home-says-tokyo-governor

[7] https://www.japantimes.co.jp/news/2017/10/16/national/tokyos-

famed-tsukiji-fish-market-moved-next-september-october/#
.WvivO0gvxPY

[8] http://www.japan-guide.com/e/e3025.html

[9]   http://www.archdaily.com/151551/the-evolution-of-the-
japanese-tea-house

[10] https://en.wikipedia.org/wiki/Chashitsu#An_ideal_tea_house

[11]http://www.seriouseats.com/2012/05/navigating-tokyo-ramen-
street-first-avenue-tokyo-station-japan-rokurinsha.html

[12]   http://www.businessinsider.com/why-so-many-vending-
machines-in-japan-2017-1

[13] https://en.wikipedia.org/wiki/Japanese_work_environment

[14]   https://www.cnbc.com/2017/03/09/heres-why-japan-is-
obsessed-with-robots.html

[15] https://stbooking.co/en/5663

[16] https://www.chowhound.com/post/japanese-slurp-noodles-
789005

[17] https://en.wikipedia.org/wiki/Shibuya

[18] https://en.wikipedia.org/wiki/Shibuya

[19] https://nerdnomads.com/hachiko_the_dog

[20] https://backpackerlee.wordpress.com/2014/01/28/a-whole-
latte-chaos-starbucks-at-shibuya/

[21] https://en.wikipedia.org/wiki/Pet_ownership_in_Japan

[22] https://whereintokyo.com/dbinx/animalcafe.html

[23] http://whereintokyo.com/venues/25239.html

[24]https://www.forbes.com/sites/geoffreymorrison/2016/05/30/the-
best-ramen-in-the-world-japans-ichiran-ramen/#1440c25828cd

5

Day 5: Farmers' Market, Pride Parade, Sweets, and a Public Bath

On the morning of the fifth day of our trip, we rushed to the train station. We only stopped at one of the stands at the station, to get a curry filled croquette (or *Korokke*) for ¥300. Curry is considered one of the most popular foods in Japan[1]. In fact, there's an entirely different curry recipe than the well-known version served in western countries, made only in Japan. Curry pastry is a convenient, and mouth-watering way to enjoy curry on the go. So, indeed we ate the croquette on our way to the train. The reason we were in a hurry was to get to the UN University farmers' market. This market only opens twice a week, on Saturday and Sunday, and offers locally grown products. We heard about this market when we were watching YouTube videos before our visit, and we were excited to add this destination to our plan. When we got there, we noticed it is much smaller than we anticipated, and the variety isn't great. However, there were a few artisan honey, nuts, and fruit stands. At one of the stands, we sampled a wonderfully sweet orange.

Around the market stands there were a variety of food trucks offering smoked meats, Japanese breakfast, and more. At one of the trucks, we purchased a Japanese omelet with Kimchi and pork, and a side salad for ¥1,000. The omelet was fluffy and full of flavor with a hint of spice from the kimchi (Kimchi is a Korean dish made from fermented cabbage). The side salad was very fresh and refreshing. The entire meal was gone in seconds.

At a different stand, we got a *hand drip* coffee, also known as *pour-over* coffee. It was the first time we came across this method of brewing coffee. This method is different from the automated brewed coffee in a sense that it is done manually. The person brewing the coffee keeps pouring water into the coffee filter until he reaches the wanted coffee amount. This is much more complex than that, and there are many websites devoted to the perfect recipes[2]. We enjoyed the coffee very much. It was strong, very invigorating, and had a hint of an orange taste.

Left: UN farmers' market. Right: hand drip coffee.

My husband and I love coffee, and we are used to drinking about two cups of coffee each day. When we were planning the trip, our friends played a prank on us and told us it is challenging to find coffee in Japan. Naively, we believed them. When we planned the trip and entered our destinations on google maps, each time we saw a coffee shop on the map near our destinations, we added it to the map. After being in Japan for only one day, it was very easy to see that finding coffee is a very small challenge. As it happens, Japan is ranked 4th for coffee consumption in the world[3]. The journey towards the 4th place began in the 1880s when the first coffee shop opened. However, back then there were restrictions over coffee import, so the industry did not advance until the 1960s[4]. Since then, the coffee industry grew exponentially, and now there are coffee shops belonging to Japanese franchises (such as Doutor), imported coffee shops (such as Starbucks), and even vending machines that sell a variety of hot and cold coffee beverages.

Tip: The UNU market is a nice stop if you are already nearby, or if you live in Tokyo and want some fresh and local products. I wouldn't recommend going out of your way to get there. It is a humble market, with nothing too special.

Our next destination was a park in *Harajuku* area, called *Yoyogi*. Yoyogi park became a public park in 1967 after the 1964 Olympics were held there[5]. The park consists of two parts: forest and stadium areas separated by a road[6]. This park isn't considered as one of the prettiest in Tokyo, but it attracts people mostly due to its vitality. It is a great place to go people watching. Especially on Sundays, the park transforms to host musicians, comedians, dancers, and cosplayers.

We decided to go to the park because it was the day on which the annual pride parade was scheduled. Every year, there is an entire week dedicated to the celebration of the lesbian, gay, bisexual, and transgender (LGBT) pride. The highlight of the festivities is the parade. Thousands of people from Japan and around the world come to participate in the parade[7]. The parade is a three kilometer walk around the Harajuku/Shibuya area[8].

When we were in the park's proximity, the streets were almost empty and very quiet. Soon enough we started hearing the faint sound of a crowd at a distance. When we arrived at the park, it felt like entering a festival. There were many people, numerous food and activity stalls, and decorations. Among the stalls, we saw one that offers taking wedding pictures and another with pride flag souvenirs. Most people were regularly dressed, but there were also a few interesting outfits (as seen in the photos below).

LGBT pride parade in Yoyogi park.

While we were deciding what we want to eat, the parade was assembling at the starting point. Many people were standing in line to be organized into the parade. The atmosphere was very cheerful. After looking at the cheerful people, we started focusing on the food. We decided to get a steamed bun, which turned out to be an excellent choice because it was one of the best buns we had so far (since it was soft, hot, and extra juicy inside). After finishing the bun and walking around the stalls, we headed towards the park's exit. On our way, we saw the parade pass with cheers and waves.

We headed towards another touristy destination: Harajuku. Harajuku is known for the shopping opportunities it offers, but it is also popular among teenagers for its extreme fashion[9]. We went to *Takeshita Dori* Street, which is where new fashion styles get formed. It is a narrow street with many shops and fast food. This street has several Japanese crepe shops that offer a huge variety of crepes filled with fruits, ice cream, chocolates, and more sweets. Besides the sweet and comforting flavors, these crepes are colorful and very esthetic. We bought a chocolate ice cream with banana and brownie filling for ¥600. The warm crepe goes so well with the ice cream. It is very easy to see why there are so many of these shops on one street, as they all get plenty of business. The downside of this street was that it was packed with people because of the holiday, so each place had lines and the movement down the street was extra slow.

We only saw one person dressed in a very peculiar outfit, as shown in the image below. This doesn't mean there weren't more people dressed in an extreme manner, but that it was so very crowded.

Tip: If you wish to see the teenage fashion figures in Harajuku, the best time to go is on Sundays. However, be aware that it is also the busiest time to be there.

Left: Takeshita Dori Street in Harajuku. Right: extreme street fashion.

The highlight of our time there was the *CROQUANT CHOU*, which is a cream puff. The store that sells these puffs (ZAKUZAKU) had the longest line that we saw, and for a reason. The line took about 15-20 minutes, but it was worth every second. The puff comes warm and crunchy with the creamiest, most delicately sweet filling. I'm only sorry we didn't get more of these while we had the chance. ¥250 is a very low price compared to the high quality of the product.

Left: sweet crepe filled with chocolate ice cream, brownie, and banana. Right: Croquant Chou (cream puff).

Contrary to what my mother used to tell me, the sweets did not ruin my appetite. We went to Harajuku Gyouzarou restaurant that offers steamed or fried gyoza for ¥290 per half a dozen. This restaurant is located in the *Cat Street* which is a shopping street said to be quieter than the surrounding streets. There, we notice a sandwich place that sells lobster sandwiches. We were already full from the gyoza, but we were eating with our eyes when we looked at the screens broadcasting the sandwiches they offer. They looked so good. Definitely a destination for our next visit.

Our friends wanted to do some shopping in Harajuku, but we were tired of the crowd. We decided to split up, so they stayed in Harajuku while we went to the subway. We got off at *Nishi-Nippori*, one station away from our hotel, to explore the area. We didn't see anything exciting. All we saw was a residential neighborhood, but being free from the crowd was worth it.

During our walk, we decided on going to a public bath, or *Sento*. Public baths are very common in Japan nowadays, but their history dates back to the 13th century when the first Sento was established[10]. In the last 100 years, the popularity of the public baths decreased, due to the increasing number of residences with baths. Nowadays, people who visit the public baths do it mainly to relax, or for social reasons (Japanese people believe that physical closeness brings emotional closeness[11]).

Good to know: Bathing in a public bath (sento) is done in the nude.

Tip: If you plan to go to a public bath, it is essential to follow the *bathing etiquette*[12] since manners and respect are very important in Japan.

Some public baths don't admit people with tattoos since tattoos are associated with criminals, gangs[13], and the *Yakuza[14]*. Yakuza is the largest organized crime syndicate in the world with more than 100,000 members[15]. The power structure of the Yakuza organization is a typical pyramid structure with a single head at the top. The rules are enforced with the use of force. For example, when a subordinate fails to accomplish a task, his punishment would be amputation of a part of the finger. Alternatively, the subordinate can amputate his own finger as a form of apology. In the old days, that meant that his ability to use his sword as protection would be inhibited and his dependence on his boss will grow deeper. In the past years, this tradition subsided since it made the identification of the Yakuza members an easy job for the police. Another Yakuza identification mark is the full-body tattoos. These tattoos are often made by hand tools (not electrical) and could take years to complete[16]. The association of tattoos with the Yakuza is the main reason that tattoos are still a taboo in Japan, and why many public baths don't allow admittance to people with tattoos.

Good to know: Some public baths sell tattoo covers for people with tattoos who want to be admitted.

We went to Saito-yu right next to our hotel. When we arrived to the entrance of the public bath, we saw a vending machine with many buttons only in Japanese. We asked at the reception for help purchasing tickets. One of the men working at the reception went with us and helped us with the vending machine. Next, we went back to the reception and gave them our tickets (¥430 per person). At this point, it was time for my husband and me to split up. I went to the women's locker room, and David went to the men's.

Good to know: The sign for the women's locker room in a public bathhouse is red, while the men's is blue.

I entered the locker room and saw there were many women around, but I was the only tourist. I went to the biggest locker because I had a lot of things with me. I took off my clothes and put everything in the locker. When I closed the door, I noticed that it only locks with a ¥100 coin. I looked in my wallet and realized I don't have any coins with me. I assumed the coin is only needed for the biggest locker, but when I looked at the smallest one it was exactly the same. Very aware I am entirely naked, I looked around and located a vending machine. I took a ¥1,000 bill out of my wallet, but then I saw the machine doesn't accept bills. Now I had a dilemma: I had a lot of money with me because the decision to go to the public bath was on the spur of the moment. On the other hand, Japan has an extremely low crime rate. I decided to leave my things in an unlocked locker.

I went to the next stop of the facility which is the showers. I almost stepped off the locker room mat onto the wet floor of the shower facilities, when I realized I don't have a towel with me. In all the videos we watched and websites we read before coming to the public bath, everyone said the towel is supplied by the facility. So, I figured I didn't see it in the locker room because I was so occupied with the matter of the coin. I went back to look in the locker, but there was no towel there or in nearby lockers. I looked for a towel stand, but to my surprise, I saw every woman around me used a different towel. Finally, it dawned on me: I was supposed to bring my own towel. I thought about going to the shower and wearing my clothes on wet skin, but the locker room was spotless, and the floor was dry so I didn't want to ruin it. Very sadly I got dressed, took all of my things with me and went to the lobby. I thought I will sit there and wait for my husband. Then, I thought that this might be my only chance to visit a public bath, and I don't want this to be how it went. With new determination, I headed to the reception and asked them if they have towels (I mimed since they didn't speak English). The receptionist smiled, nodded his head and took me back to the vending machine at the entrance. There he pushed a button in Japanese, I handed him my ¥1,000 bill, and he handed me a towel and a handful of change. With this new triumphant feeling, I returned to the locker room and got the biggest locker to close.

My husband had a very similar experience: at some point, he noticed that he doesn't have a towel. Unfortunately for him, this moment was while he was standing wet and naked in a room full of people after he already finished showering and taking a bath. On the way back to the locker room, he looked around and found a new and dry towel. He thought it was for the guests of the public bath, so he used it. When I told him about my experience with the towel, I saw all the color in his face fade away. Only at this moment, he realized he stole someone else's towel!

Before going to the bath area, you need to wash yourself in the shower room, so you will be clean when you enter the bath. The shower room is basically a line of faucets at mid-human height level without any partition in between them. Next to each faucet, there are soap and shampoo bottles, a basin, and a stool. Since there is no partition between the faucet stations, each bather is supposed to sit on the stool and use the basin to water himself. The reason for this way of bathing is that it is considered very rude to splash water at someone else. After completely washing the entire body, the bather is supposed to wash the bathing station, so it will be clean for the next person.

Tip: Before entering a public bath, it is important to make sure your hair doesn't touch the water, so make sure you bring a hair tie with you.

Good to know: You are expected to keep your towel balanced on your head while you are in the bath (at a public bathhouse). It is extremely rude to let your towel touch the water.

Next stop is the baths. When I entered the bath area, I noticed there were four baths. Each one had a different shape and temperature. The first bath I saw was very crowded, probably because it had the most pleasant water temperature. As I mentioned before, the bathing is done in the nude, so I felt a little strange entering a crowded bath. I decided to skip this one and continued to the next one. The sign to the second one warned that the water is very hot, so I skipped this one as well. The sign of the third bath read "electric bath." I looked at it and it seemed like a regular hot tub. It had air jets, and there were bathers inside. I decided this was a good choice, so I entered.

One of the air jet spots was vacant, so I went there. It was very nice, but after five minutes or so I became extremely warm. Usually when I go into a hot tub, when I get too warm I just sit on the edge with my legs inside. However, this was definitely not the right place to do that. I got out to check the fourth bath. The sign read "cold bath." I didn't believe it and tried for myself. I gave quite a performance for one Japanese lady who noticed how quickly I got in and out of there.

After cooling so rapidly, I had built a new tolerance for the warmth of the "electric bath." When I got there, my spot was taken and I had to go to a different area of the bath. I went to one corner, but as soon as I got there I felt electrical shocks! I jumped away from this corner as quickly as I could. Turns out it was really an electrical bath. I started thinking this public bath experience adds much more stress than it's relieving. Slowly cooking in the middle of the electric bath, I noticed there is a door that leads to an open-air bath. I went exploring once more. The door opened to reveal a medium sized bath in the middle of a fenced yard. I entered it and noticed the water was exactly at the right temperature. The fresh air, along with the warm water, relieved all of my stress away. Thinking back on this experience, I can finally understand how Goldilocks felt when she finally found the right bed.

I found one explanation for the electric bath, but it hasn't been scientifically proven. It's supposedly useful for stretching your muscles[17].

It was raining when my husband and I exited the sento, so we sat on a bench at the entrance waiting for the rain to stop. Two minutes or so passed, and a sento worker ran outside with a bin full of umbrellas. We took a random one and left. Now, don't think we are thieves who enjoy stealing umbrellas and towels. Umbrellas in Japan are considered a cheap and disposable item.

Most umbrellas in Japan are made from transparent plastic and look the same. Since most establishments demand to leave your umbrella at a stand near the entrance, it is prevalent to take someone else's umbrella when you go. Moreover, most Japanese people don't think stealing an umbrella hurts someone. Likewise, they are not offended when their umbrella gets taken[18]. On the other hand, they probably do get upset if their towel gets stolen, but in my husband's defense, it was an honest mistake.

The public bath opened up our pores, but also our appetites. We went to a convenience store next to our hotel. We got a small sushi bento box for 20% off, and a rice cracker package (*senbei*) for ¥170. The crackers were great, but the sushi was definitely a letdown. Maybe the last sushi we ate made us spoiled, but the discounted sushi tasted cheap.

Rice crackers, or *senbei*, are crunchy crackers made of non-sticky rice dough[19]. The early version of the senbei originated during the 700s. The first senbei was made of grain flour and wasn't crunchy. Nowadays, the rice senbei comes in two main variations: baked and fried. For both varieties, soy sauce is the main ingredient that gives the cracker its umami flavor. Soy sauce originally came to Japan from China and was somewhere between a modern soy sauce and miso paste[20]. In 1254, when the Zen monk Kakushin came back from China, he began making miso paste. While making the miso paste he noticed that the liquid he gets also tastes delicious. This was the beginning of the tamari soy sauce.

本体価格
より

20 %引

今が
お買得

698 円

③⓪ 盛り合わせ（４点盛り）
白　身（　ぶ　り　）

Discounted sushi from a convenience store.

We rested for a while in our room, and then we went for some Yakitori at a tiny Izakaya next to our previous hotel. We wanted to go to this place because we have passed next to it every evening and never went inside. The Izakaya had precisely five seats: four for us, and one for the person who was already enjoying what I can only assume was his fifth drink. This person was very cheerful and had a strong aroma of alcohol. His lack of English knowledge did not stop him from trying to speak with us. It was both a bit disturbing and endearing. He told us he is a salaryman, and we talked about our plans for the travel in Japan.

The Izakaya had all menu items written in Japanese on the wall. The owner of the Izakaya showed us which items are chicken, beef, and pork. We ordered random items, and we got meatballs, chicken skin, chicken and leek, chicken liver, beef strips, and pork belly. We also ordered plum wine and whiskey for a total of ¥3,700 per couple. I can't say any of the skewers were too memorable. The awkward thing was, when we ordered chicken liver, our friend asked the cook not to overcook it. I think the cook was very offended. As was previously said, Japanese people take their work very seriously. They train for years before they are satisfied with their own work.

Tip: Don't tell Japanese people how to do their jobs. Otherwise, they will be highly offended.

As we were sitting in the Izakaya, suddenly my husband and I remembered we left something in the refrigerator of our previous hotel room. Since we were nearby, my husband went to the reception to ask if they found something in our fridge. The receptionist went to the back and brought a neat package that contained my book (that I didn't even know was missing) and a bottle of lychee liqueur we left there. They said they had to dispose of the open food item for sanitary reasons. We were amazed about the package and care they gave to our forgotten items. It was almost as if we received a present that contained a book and a liqueur. This just shows how attentive to details Japanese people are.

Sources:

[1] https://en.wikipedia.org/wiki/Japanese_curry

[2] https://coffee-brewing-methods.com/how-to-make-pour-over-coffee-at-home/

[3] https://matcha-jp.com/en/2561

[4] http://www.dannychoo.com/en/post/26955/Japan+Coffee+Culture.html

[5] http://www.japan-guide.com/e/e3034_002.html

[6] https://tokyocheapo.com/lifestyle/cheapo-guide-yoyogi-park/

[7] https://www.timeout.com/tokyo/lgbt/tokyo-rainbow-pride-2017

[8] https://tokyocheapo.com/events/tokyo-rainbow-pride/

[9] http://www.japan-guide.com/e/e3006.html

[10] http://japan-magazine.jnto.go.jp/en/1502_sento.html

[11] https://en.wikipedia.org/wiki/Sent%C5%8D

[12] http://www.sentoguide.info/etiquette

[13] https://www.japanbaths.com/the-way-of-the-sento/tattoos-in-japanese-public-baths/

[14] https://en.wikipedia.org/wiki/Irezumi

[15] https://thoughtcatalog.com/michael-koh/2014/02/15-scary-things-you-didnt-know-about-the-yakuza/

[16] https://en.wikipedia.org/wiki/Irezumi

[17]   https://www.japanbaths.com/faq/whats-the-deal-with-electric-baths/

[18] http://www.okwave.com/en/culturezine/psychological_analyses/1184/1184/en

[19] https://matcha-jp.com/en/2024

[20] https://soysauce.or.jp/en/history/

6

Day 6: Traditional Theatre, Japanese Schnitzel, Kitchen Town, and More Food

When we left the hotel in the morning, we got to a small crosswalk that had four traffic officers responsible for controlling the traffic. The amazing thing was that even though it was an utterly insignificant crosswalk with only the four of us crossing, each one of them directed us at the same time. There weren't even any cars near us. This just shows you how much integrity Japanese people have. If they are given a job, they will fulfill it to the best of their ability. In any other place I've ever visited, given the same situation, only one officer would direct the traffic while the rest would talk amongst themselves or be otherwise occupied.

We really wanted to start the morning with some sushi as we did two days ago. The only problem was that all the sushi restaurants around us were still closed. Even after we gave up on the sushi idea, we still couldn't find anything good open in the morning. The earliest most restaurants in the area open is around 11AM. Defeated, we decided to go to the subway and get something there. My husband and I got a pack with three sandwiches for ¥560. The sandwiches were surprisingly not half bad. The package included tuna, omelet, and ham sandwiches. We ate the sandwiches and hopped on a train to *Higashi-Ginza* to go to a traditional Japanese theatre (or *Kabuki*) at *Kabukiza Theatre.*

Kabukiza Theatre.

Originated in 1603[1], Kabuki used to be performed only by women mostly in front of common people[2]. During the Edo period, women were banned from acting and from this point up to now, all the roles are played by men. Usually, young adolescent men are selected to play female characters, due to their less masculine features. Kabuki entails appealing costumes, striking makeup, and exaggerated movements which help the audience understand the plot since the language spoken is an old-fashioned Japanese, not commonly used nowadays. The music during the play is performed by traditional musical instruments. The props and scenery are moved by performers dressed in black called *Kurogo*, who don't play an active role in the performance.

A full Kabuki play can consist of three or four acts over 4-5 hours.

A ticket for the entire show can be sold for up to ¥20,000[3], while there are discounted tickets for a single act. The show we came to see started at 11AM, but discounted tickets for a single act (¥1,500) were sold starting from 10:30AM. At Kabukiza there are only 150 discounted tickets in total: 90 top row seats and 60 standing spots.

Tip: The discounted tickets for a *Kabuki* play at *Kabukiza Theatre* don't come with assigned seats, so it is recommended to arrive earlier to get a seat. We came at 10AM, and while there were many people in front of us, we got seats.

At 10AM there was already a line to the cashier, even though he still didn't begin selling the discounted tickets. When the clock stroke 10:30AM, the line immediately started moving with an impressing speed. We got our tickets and entered to find seats. The hall wasn't too big, but it was very appealing. One interesting thing I noticed was that women left their purses on the seats and went outside without a worry that someone would steal their belongings or even their place. As I mentioned before, this is because the crime rate in Japan is extremely low (one of the lowest in the world[4]).

We didn't know anything about kabuki plays before we went there. In my mind, I imagined there would be many dance, song, and battle scenes during the play. 10 minutes into the show I realized it is not at all as I imagined it to be. While the scenery, actors, costumes, and music were of very high quality, most of the time the actors were immobile and only spoke. Our lack of knowledge and haste to get seats prevented us from getting a small screen with English subtitles. Consequently, most of the show was very unclear for us.

My luck was that a person sitting one row in front of me had a screen with English subtitles, large enough for me to see. When the act ended, we went outside, and our friend said he was disappointed because he didn't understand anything. I decided to prank him and said that it's strange because I followed almost all of it. He was amazed and asked me to tell the story.

* Spoiler alert*
The story is about a sword maker who wants to sell a sword he made to give the money to his son-in-law. The buyers didn't believe the sword was any good, so they demanded proof. They wanted him to prove the sword was good enough to cut people in half, so he volunteered his body as proof. Most of the act was leading to this crucial test when the daughter of the sword maker (played by a male actor) was pleading for his life.

My friend has already joked around that I secretly speak Japanese, but at this moment he was left speechless. Sadly for me, his sharp wife realized I saw someone else's screen and unveiled my prank. In my opinion, the Kabuki is indeed a unique experience, but I won't be coming for more than one act.

Tip: If you are planning to go to a *Kabuki* play, I recommend getting a screen with subtitles when you purchase the tickets.

We went to the basement souvenir shop. There are many souvenirs to choose from: kimonos (traditional garment), hair accessories, or even candies. We got candies with bits of salt inside, packed in a decorated box. Also, I purchased a *Kanzashi* (an ornamental hair stick) decorated with Sakura flowers. I was very thrilled I found it at a reasonable price (¥1,000) because I saw it at a different attraction for four times as much.

The origin of Kanzashi dates back to ancient Japan when it was believed that sticks could defend against evil spirits[5]. To have this protection, people used to put sticks in their hair. In the Nara period (710-794 AD) the Kanzashi was brought to Japan from China. During the Edo period, hairstyles became more complicated and demanded a larger number of Kanzashi. As a result, new designs were invented, including Kanzashi used as a concealed weapon. Nowadays, Kanzashi is mainly worn by brides, geishas, maikos, or by adepts in a tea ceremony. However, some young women wear it as a fashion statement. Traditionally, by the number and location of the Kanzashi, a woman can indicate her status.

We became hungry, so we decided to go for lunch. We wanted to try a new Japanese favorite: the Japanese schnitzel (breaded and fried flattened meat), or *Tonkatsu*. Tonkatsu is deep-fried breaded pork. Usually, it is served with a hearty portion of shredded cabbage and a Tonkatsu sauce. Tonkatsu was invented in 1899 as a Japanese version of the European cuisine. Before 1899, there was a similar version made of beef, but it wasn't deep-fried[6].

We went to *Nishimura* restaurant, located right next to the Kabukiza theatre. Only problem was we came precisely at the lunch rush hour. There was a long line of people waiting to be seated at one of the seats around the counter. Almost all the people I looked at were devouring the Tonkatsu so quickly, it was unclear if it's because it was so good or because they were in a hurry to get back to work. Probably both, but I was sure about the quality of the food when I saw the bare plates on their way back to the kitchen. As the line was moving, my hunger and expectation increased. When we were seated, we noticed only four people were working behind the counter. We were impressed with the speed at which they worked and with the uncompromised quality of the food coming to every customer. The restaurant has a family feel to it. It only serves Tonkatsu, and the only variety is in the pork cut. We ordered the most expensive one (¥1,400) which is also the fattiest piece.

81

Tunkatsu meal at Nishimura restaurant.

After approximately a five-minute wait, we got a tray overflowing with food. You can almost become full just by looking at it. Almost. We received the Tonkatsu with a giant pile of shredded cabbage, pork soup, and rice. It was very fresh and hearty. I especially liked the soup, but it was too fatty for my husband. It amazes me that people can work after eating such a heavy meal. We tried to eat quickly, so people wouldn't be late for work, but it was somewhat challenging eating this massive portion in a hurry.

Tip: I would suggest avoiding the lunch hour rush to have a more enjoyable experience at popular restaurants.

After lunch, our friends wanted to go to *Shin Okubo* Korean town, located in Shinjuku, while we wanted to go to *Kappabashi*. We decided to split up once more, and meetup in the evening. Kappabashi Street, also referred to as the "kitchen town," is a street full of shops selling restaurant supplies[7]. These supplies include cooking utensils, knives, chairs, plastic foods, etc. We came to Japan with a mission to purchase good quality Japanese knives for cooking. If you only plan to be in Tokyo, this is an excellent place for that. We, however, knew we were going to visit Kyoto and Osaka, so we decided to hold off on the purchase to get a better deal. Regardless, it's a great place for souvenir shopping or even for window shopping. We found a few great items to purchase, including wooden bowls for Ramen. We couldn't believe it when we looked at our watch and found out we spent three hours shopping there. I am not sure if it was because we love kitchen items so much or because it was one of the less crowded spots we came across in Tokyo.

Good to know: Kappabashi shopping street usually operates between 9AM-5PM.

There are many unique restaurant supplies you can find in this lovely street. Amongst them, there are *Noren* curtains. Noren curtains were initially used by private homes and businesses in Japan as a fabric divider between rooms or between the indoors and the outdoors[8]. They have a rectangular shape with vertical slits, and nowadays they are used to display the logos of businesses. Besides its advertisement role, the Noren is also used to block the sun, wind, and dust from reaching the indoors. Some claim they are also used to build the curiosity of people passing by the veiled interior of a restaurant or shop[9].

In the middle of the Kappabashi street, there is a tiny alley with a golden statue of a marine creature that looks like a cross between a human and a frog holding a fish in one hand and a pole in the other. This statue is a statue of *Kappa*, a Japanese folklore character. Kappa is said to be based on a giant salamander that grabs its prey with its claws. It usually thought to have an attitude of a trickster, and it is used as a warning for children against the dangers in the rivers and lakes[10].

Left: chopstick rests sold in Kappabashi street. Right: Kappa statue.

Kappabashi is located only 30 minutes walk away from our hotel, so we decided to walk to our hotel and explore this part of the city. On our way, we passed next to *Uguisudani* station. We saw a very lively Yakitori spot right next to the station, but the line was too long for us. We stood near it people watching. It looked like a regular spot for people on their way home from work. Next, we went on a bridge above the station. The bridge offers a lovely view of the passing trains. It was already past 5PM, and the sun rays were coming at an angle which gave the trains a mesmerizing look.

We kept walking towards the hotel and realized we haven't eaten for a while. We were set on finding a restaurant that serves eel, since my husband loves eel, and we didn't have any yet. We came across *Sukiya* restaurant which had a picture of an eel meal on the door. We came inside and ordered an eel meal for my husband and a Japanese beef curry for me. Maybe two minutes passed before we received our food. Turns out Sukiya is a very well-liked restaurant chain in Japan, with about 2,000 locations nationwide[11]. It looks like a fast food restaurant, but the food tasted like it came from a high-end restaurant.

The eel was very soft, and it came with Teriyaki sauce on rice. My husband claims it's the best eel he had ever had. My meal was a Japanese beef curry with rice, with a side of Miso soup and pickles. The curry was amazing. It was so creamy and delicious. I finished it to the last drop. We left the place completely full and content, after spending a symbolic ¥1,670 for the both of us.

Left: eel meal. Right: Japanese beef curry at Sukiya restaurant.

Our next stop was *Love* café and bar. We came around 6PM and were the only customers there. We sat at a tiny table on the sidewalk and listened to the vibrant remix music playing. The place was nothing special, but it had fantastic Wi-Fi. I have been struggling to upload pictures from the trip to my Google Drive, and finally, I had a chance to upload the majority of them.

When we arrived at the hotel and rejoined our friends, they told us about their day. One of the places they visited was a store that sells *origami* paper (for paper folding art). They said the shop worker gave them a few origami cranes, one of which they gave us.

It is not clear when origami was first developed, but it is known that it was invented as an art form in Japan[12]. Initially, it was only practiced by a few, mostly for religious purposes. When paper became more available, the origami became an art practiced by the masses.

We went to a restaurant near the hotel to try another Japanese classic: *Soba* noodles. Soba noodles are thin noodles made from buckwheat flour and could either be served warm or cold. During the Edo period, Soba noodles started gaining vast popularity, after it was found that a diet mainly focused on white rice may lead to Beriberi disease (caused by vitamin B1 deficiency)[13].

At the restaurant, we got a Tsukidashi minced raw fish and toasted Nori seaweeds. It looked beautiful and tasted even better. That was a promising beginning to the meal, or so we thought. When we got the Soba, we were excited, because it was also very appealing. Unfortunately, that is all it was. It was very tasteless, like eating cold noodles straight from the fridge. Seeing this was our last night in Tokyo, we decided this wasn't the way we want it to end. We took the subway and headed toward *Keisei Ueno* station in a search for a proper meal.

Left: Tsukidashi minced raw fish. Right: soba noodles.

Near Ueno station, we entered <u>Sushi Zanmai</u>. The restaurant offers sushi with prices ranging from approximately ¥100 to ¥500 per unit. There are also combinations available at decent prices. My husband and I got two fatty tuna nigiri and two Uni (sea urchin). The first time we tried Uni was at the conveyor belt, and it was very disappointing.

I was expecting it to be much better, so I decided we should try it again. I have to say that it was worth the high price (¥498). It was so amazing. It reminded me of the first time I tried oysters. It has an unusual texture, but incredible flavor. We also got a tuna set, that has 13 sushi made from different tuna cuts that come with a side of miso soup. The meal was perfect. It was a great place to have our last dinner in Tokyo. We ended up paying approximately ¥4,800 per couple, and it was worth every penny. While we were paying, we received sushi-shaped sweets on a stick- a very sweet souvenir.

Left: Uni sushi. Right: a tuna set meal at Sushi Zanmai restaurant.

Right before arriving at the hotel, we stopped for ice cream at the grocery store. I bought myself a mochi ice cream. It was so good... The box I purchased had two vanilla ice cream balls with a mochi coating. To eat them, you simply insert a popsicle stick (provided in the box) into the center of the ice cream ball and pick it up. It is both fun and delicious.

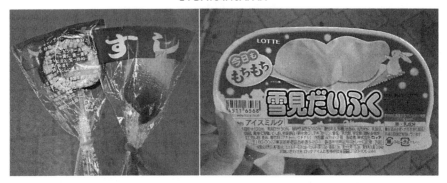

Left: sushi-shaped candy. Right: mochi ice cream.

When we got to our hotel, we went to the reception to get information about a service we heard many hotels in Japan offer: luggage delivery. This delivery service is called *Takuhaibin*. Takuhaibin is a convenient service for sending parcels and luggage from door to door nationwide*[14]*. The parcel could either be sent from your home, from a hotel, or even from some souvenir shops. The nice thing is that the item could also be delivered to a variety of locations: to a home, hotel, airport, train station, office, or a convenience store. Delivery is usually on the next day, and costs are moderate. This fantastic service is available since the 1970s.

The hotel we stayed at provides this service. We sent our luggage to a hotel in Kyoto, where we planned to stay for a few days. We were left with our carry-on luggage and a backpack filled with enough items to last us for the next couple of days.

Tip: Instead of traveling with your luggage between different cities, send it to your destination hotel with the luggage delivery service. Ask the front desk of your hotel for more information.

Tip: If you intend to send luggage to a hotel, make sure to contact the hotel before doing so. Not all hotels may be able to accept deliveries due to lack of storage space[15].

Sources:

[1] https://en.wikipedia.org/wiki/Kabuki

[2] https://www.japan-guide.com/e/e2090.html

[3] https://blog.gaijinpot.com/kabukiza-theater-tickets/

[4] http://www.nationmaster.com/blog/?p=74

[5] https://en.wikipedia.org/wiki/Kanzashi

[6] http://upbproducts.co.uk/blog/history-katsu-tonkatsu-curry/

[7] https://www.japan-guide.com/e/e3020.html

[8] https://en.wikipedia.org/wiki/Noren

[9]https://www.japantimes.co.jp/life/2017/01/14/style/curtain-call-examining-evolution-japans-humble-noren/#.WkdaqVWWaUl

[10] https://en.wikipedia.org/wiki/Kappa_(folklore)

[11] https://www.sukiya.jp/en/whats_sukiya/

[12] https://www.thesprucecrafts.com/brief-history-of-origami-2540653

[13] https://en.wikipedia.org/wiki/Soba

[14] https://www.japan-guide.com/e/e2278.html

[15] https://www.japan-guide.com/e/e2278.html

7

Day 7: Scenic Bus Drive, Kaiseki Dinner, and Private Outdoor Bath

Our plans for day 7 included a long drive to Hirayu *Onsen.* An onsen is a Japanese hot spring, said to cure skin disease and improve resistance to cold[1]. One of the reasons we chose this town is because it is conveniently located on the way from Tokyo to Takayama, which was our next destination. When we were still at home, we looked online for the best ways to get there by public transport. We found an express bus that departs from Shinjuku terminal in Tokyo at 11:05 AM and arrives in Hirayu in four and a half hours (for a total of ¥11,720 per couple). The scary part for me was when we paid for the tickets we got a message saying we'll receive the tickets via email on the morning of our trip. In my mind I ran all the scenarios that could make this day a disaster: what if the email doesn't arrive, and they don't let us board the bus without the tickets? What if we can't take one of the next buses because they are completely booked? Etc.

This brings us to the morning of day 7. My husband and I woke up early and headed straight to the train station to catch a train to Shinjuku. We wanted to avoid the rush hour, so we decided not to waste time looking for breakfast. Our friends didn't want to wait so long at the bus terminal, so they stayed for breakfast near the hotel.

Our way to the bus terminal was so lovely. I was pleased that we sent our luggage the day before, so we didn't have to carry it with us. We arrived at Shinjuku station and went to the bus terminal to look for the platform we would depart from in a few hours. Locating the place was very straightforward. So, we found the bus platform, but still hadn't received the tickets by email. To distract me from my stress, and because we were hungry, we went in a search for food.

The bus station had a convenience store, but no cafés/restaurants, so we walked back towards the train station to *NewoMan* food hall. Unfortunately, we didn't see anything exciting there either. We went to *Verve Coffee Roasters* where we got a croissant and a hand drip coffee. In a word it was meh, but at least we weren't as hungry as before. While we were sitting there, we received the email with our bus tickets. Finally, I could relax, or so I thought.

We were still hungry, so our search for food continued. We went to a mall right next to the station and headed towards the food hall. To our great disappointment, everything was still closed since it was still very early. We went to another café in the food hall called *Sawa Mura*, bought a pack of four sandwiches, and then returned to the bus station because there wasn't anything better to do. Once back at the bus station, we went to the convenience store we saw earlier and got supplies for the trip. We bought a few *Onigiris* with different fillings. Onigiri is a rice ball (or triangle) wrapped with seaweed[2]. Although the origin of the onigiri isn't clear, it is at least 2,000 years old[3]. Before the *Nara period*, rice was often shaped into small balls for eating convenience. This was before the invention of the chopsticks. Up to the *Heian period*, onigiri was called *Tonjiki*, and it had a round shape. Their shape was changed to a triangle or rectangle so they could be easily piled on a plate. Their popularity until this day stems from their simple good flavor, and because they are easily carried and eaten on-the-go.

Left: hand drip coffee at Verve Coffee Roasters. Right: sandwiches at Sawa Mura cafe.

After we finished shopping, we went to the platform. Ten minutes later, our friends joined us. A few minutes before departure time, my husband and our friend left to visit the lavatory. Five minutes before the departure time, the bus arrived, and the driver stood next to the door with a list of passengers. My friend put her luggage in the trunk, while all the passengers boarded the bus. Two minutes remained until departure, and still no sign from our husbands. The driver was looking at us uneasily, while we were looking at each other reassuringly. One long minute passed, and we heard a loud sound of people running. Thankfully, it was them. We boarded the bus, and before we settled in our seats, the bus was already moving.

This long bus ride came at the perfect timing. My feet were killing me after all the walking during the past 5 days. On average, we walked 13 km per day. During the drive, I planned to catch up on my writing and on some sleep, but as soon as we left the city these plans were abandoned. The bus ride turned out to be an attraction by itself. We drove through such amazing scenery that I was fascinated by the view from the window. We passed through rural territories and stunning green landscapes. Besides the stunning views, the nice thing about the bus ride was the stops. Although the bus is equipped with a lavatory, the bus stops twice during the drive. It was very satisfying to step outside for some fresh air and leg stretching.

One of the places we drove by was lake *Suwa*. Lake Suwa has a natural hot spring under its surface and is famous for a phenomenon called the "god's crossing" (*Omiwatari*)[4]. Omiwatari occurs during the winter when the top of the lake freezes. The hot spring water under the icy surface keeps the water circulating and creates pressure on the surface. This pressure builds up until relieved by the creation of ridges on the icy surface. These ridges can grow up to 30 cm in height and appear like tiny mountains atop a frozen lake. There are several more explanations of the phenomena. In Shinto, the frozen ridges are believed to be left by the gods after they crossed the lake. Whereas folklore says, the ridges are the trail left by the guardian god of Suwa, *Takeminakata-no-kami*, after he crosses the frozen lake to meet with his wife (*Yasakatome*) on the opposite bank[5].

The god's crossing is also famous for one more reason. The frozen ridges have been studied since the 14th century as a way to predict the crop harvest of the following year. This makes lake Suwa the first place where the weather forecast was ever used[6].

Next, we saw a very pretty dam from our window. I am not sure which dam it was since there are more than forty dams throughout the country[7]. A few minutes after passing the dam, we saw a monkey casually walking on the side of the road. It wasn't until after seeing the monkey that we saw a sign alerting to monkeys in the area. As we got closer to our destination, the temperature dropped, and we started noticing Sakura trees still in full bloom. I was so excited because the bloom was already gone when we visited Tokyo. Sakura blossom is absolutely beautiful.

A bus isn't the only way to travel in Japan. Japan is known for its high-speed bullet train (*Shinkansen*). This train reaches speeds up to 320 kilometers per hour and covers the country from north to south[8].

Good to know: There is a discounted rail pass available for tourists. This rail pass has to be purchased from outside of Japan. You may find the full information here: www.japanrailpass.net. We decided not to purchase the pass because all the bus tickets we bought ended up being cheaper than the pass.

Finally, we arrived at Hirayu bus stop. The first thing we noticed when we exited the bus was a foot onsen right inside the bus stop. What a lovely way to wait for your bus! It was very clear from the first minute we arrived that we were in an area famous for its onsens.

Left: water wheel fountain in Hirayu. Right: foot onsen at Hirayu bus stop.

Hirayu is located in Okuhida, a region of Gifu Prefecture (jurisdiction), located in the Northern Japan Alps[9]. Hirayu is the largest and oldest town in Okuhida. It has many onsens, and it's also home to many *ryokans*. A ryokan is a traditional Japanese inn. Its origin dates back to the 8th century when the oldest hotel in the world was established[10]. The traditional and old-fashioned nature of the ryokan is the reason why it's rare to find it in big cities. They are usually more expensive compared to other hotels, so they aren't an obvious choice for the budget traveler; however, the luxury and character of the ryokan makes it an ideal fit for scenic sites. Indeed, most ryokans are located close to seashores or mountains.

The guest rooms in a ryokan have a traditional style with sliding doors and *Tatami* mats. Tatami mats are traditional mats made of rush grass and rice straw. They are made from natural materials and are less damaging to knees, back, and joints than a regular floor[11]. They act as insulators, so they keep rooms warm in the winter and cool during the summer. Moreover, they purify the air by absorbing nitrogen dioxide and control the humidity of the room. The bed in a ryokan is also a traditional futon bed. Most ryokans offer public baths with hot spring water from the area, and a few offer private hot spring baths.

After the long bus ride, we were eager to finally see the room we booked in Nakamurakan Ryokan. Luckily, the Ryokan was only a 5 min walk from the bus station. We chose this Ryokan because the location was great, the price was decent (¥24,840 per room per night), but mostly because they offered a private hot spring bath. The private bath was available for an entire night for only ¥1,000. The problem was, they only have three private baths, so we were determined to book them in advance. However, finding a way to contact them was a bit challenging. Thankfully, Google offers an excellent service for translating entire web pages. So, although this was challenging, it wasn't impossible. I found the hotel's email address (onsen@fine.ocn.ne.jp) and sent them the following request: "Is it possible for us to make a reservation for the Private Open-air Bath in advance? We are very excited to visit the bath, and we don't want to miss it". As a reply I received the funniest email:

"Hello,

Canada

Thank you for a reservation of 5/9.

Because it is two sets by couple plan, will it be to want to borrow two private buses?

It is 1,000 yen X2=2,000 yen with two.

I prepare.

I wait.

Nakamurakan"

I understood that since we booked two rooms, they asked if we want two private baths for a total of ¥2,000. I replied that yes, this is precisely what we wanted.

When we got to the ryokan, we made sure we booked the two baths with the reception desk clerk (who surprisingly spoke excellent English). The interior of the ryokan seemed so much larger than it did from outside. A junior worker of the ryokan led us to our rooms and showed us the hotel facilities on the way. We entered the room's *Genkan*, or foyer, which was a step-down from the entrance. The genkan is the space where you leave your outdoor shoes and exchange them for slippers to be worn inside the room. The room had different subsections. There was a tea area with floor seats and a tea set. Right next to it we saw two futons with a warm blanket and rice pillows. On the other side of the room there was a cozy indoor veranda, and finally, there was a bathroom area.

When we finished exploring the rooms, we explored the rest of the ryokan. The ryokan was decorated similarly to a deluxe hunting cabin. It had many displays of taxidermy animals dressed and posed to tell a story. On the other hand, there were many carved wood furniture and statues that gave the ryokan a more luxurious look. The table in the lobby was particularly astounding to me. It was entirely carved with fantastic detail. One corner of the table had a carving of a tiger with a fur that seemed soft to the touch.

Left: futon beds. Right: taxidermy animal display at Nakamurakan ryokan.

While my husband and friends were getting ready, I went outside to wait for them. Right in front of the hotel entrance I noticed a tiny waterfall that pours its hot spring water into a man-made foot onsen. Next to it was a bench with a curved and bumpy backrest for stress relief. Also, there was a foot chi path to relieve stress in the entire body through the feet. The air outside was chilly, and the hot steam rising from the foot onsen, along with the relaxing sound of the water relieved all the stress I had. I sat on the curved bench and followed the instructions displayed on a sign next to it to reach a total state of serenity.

The carved table at Nakamurakan ryokan.

My friends and husband joined me, and we went to café Mustache where we ordered our first Japanese *siphon* coffee. Siphon coffee was invented in the 1830s and is still made in many cafés in Japan. This coffee maker consists of two chambers where the lower chamber contains the water and the upper chamber includes a filter and ground coffee. When the water is boiling, the vapor pressure pushes the water to the upper chamber where the water is mixed with the coffee. When the heat source is removed, and the coffee is cooled down, gravity sends the coffee through the filter and back to the lower chamber[12]. The entire process looks a lot like a chemical experiment done in a lab.

We took our siphon coffees to go because we were in a hurry to get to a steamed bun stand we saw at the bus stop. The stand had a special steamed bun: instead of the usual pork stuffing, they offered Hida beef stuffing. Unfortunately, we reached the stand five minutes after closing time, and the vendor was already gone. We also planned to go to the Hirayu Grand Waterfall (Hirayu Otaki)[13] that's only a 20-minute walk from the ryokan. Sadly, it was getting cold and dark, so we decided not to go.

My husband took these two consecutive defeats to heart. He was very upset that we didn't buy the bun when we got off the bus as he suggested. We decided to take a walk around the hotel instead, and the path led us back to the foot onsen and the tiny waterfall. We decided to stay there until dinner.

We removed our shoes and dipped our feet in the foot onsen. The water was very warm, and as you get closer to the tiny waterfall the temperature increases. The warm vapor had a smell of Sulfur, but it didn't affect our experience at all. I could see that after two minutes my husband was smiling and content. The relaxing onsen did its job and lifted our spirits.

Left: a bench with a curved and bumpy backrest for stress relief. Right: a foot onsen near Nakamurakan ryokan.

Right before dinner, we changed our clothes to *Yukatas*. A yukata is a traditional costume, similar to a kimono but more casual[14]. Many ryokans provide guests with a yukata to be worn in all hotel facilities. The yukata set consists of a yukata, a belt (*obi*), and a coat. Some ryokans also provide guests with socks and wooden slippers.

Festively dressed, we headed to the food hall for a *kaiseki* dinner. Although a kaiseki dinner looks like a multi-course gourmet dinner, there is much more to it than that[15]. First, the purpose of the kaiseki is to convey respect and hospitality to the guest since initially, it used to be only presented to the noble class. Second, a true kaiseki dinner follows the *shun* principle. The shun principle dictates that the ingredients used for the meal should be at the peak of their freshness and as natural as possible[16]. To achieve the shun principle a kaiseki chef chooses local and seasonal ingredients to form a memorable story about the specific time and place of the meal. Lastly, each detail, from the cutlery and table cover up to a single decorative fresh herb, is organized in the most artistic and eye-pleasing way imaginable.

Each kaiseki dinner varies between different chefs and seasons. However, there are some standard components, such as an appetizer

(*Sakizuze*), seasonal sashimi (*Mukōzuke*), a dish with a lid (*Futa-mono*), pickled vegetables (*Kō no mono*), miso soup, and dessert (*Mizumono*)[17].

When we entered the dining hall, our table was already set with many small dishes. Some of the dishes were covered with lids, while the rest presented a lovely image of texture and color. Each course was completely different than the next and very attractive. As for the taste, I believe the food was made at a very high quality, but the flavors are very different than the modern palate. There were a few components I enjoyed, like the miso soup, sashimi, sausages, and pie. There were also unusual new flavors. For example, there was a hard-boiled egg that was cooked in the onsen water. It had a very different taste and texture than I'm used to. Although I wholeheartedly believe the kaiseki dinner at the Nakamurakan was of a very high quality and observed the shun rules to the letter, I was left disappointed. Probably because I was expecting more familiar tastes and textures. That being said, I regret nothing. The overall experience was absolutely one of a kind.

Kaiseki dinner at Nakamurakan ryokan.

We returned to our rooms for a short rest before our next new experience at the private outdoor bath. After 15 minutes we left our room and went to the dressing room that leads to the bath. After we finished getting ready, we opened the door that leads to the bath without knowing what to expect. A chilly wind greeted our faces while we were trying to observe every detail of the fenced private bath. We didn't have long to observe since it was cold, and we were naked.

We entered the bath slowly and felt the moss-covered stones at our feet. The bath was just warm enough to not feel cold. Around us the night was quiet, and it felt luxurious to have the bath all to ourselves. While we were sitting there, a light rain began to pour. It just enhanced the romantic and unique experience.

After enjoying the bath, we returned to our room and went to bed. I was worried it would be difficult for me to fall asleep on the rice pillow. I lay on the bed and thought about the unusual day I had, and before I realized, I drifted off to sleep.

Sources:
[1] https://www.japan-guide.com/e/e5942.html

[2] https://en.wikipedia.org/wiki/Onigiri

[3] http://www.iromegane.com/japan/vocabulary/history-of-onigiri/

[4] https://blog.gaijinpot.com/lake-suwa-gods-crossing/

[5] https://en.wikipedia.org/wiki/Lake_Suwa

[6] https://blog.gaijinpot.com/lake-suwa-gods-crossing/

[7] http://damnet.or.jp/cgi-bin/binranA/enTableAllItiran.cgi?al=A

[8] https://www.japanstation.com/shinkansen-high-speed-train-network-in-japan/

[9] https://www.japan-guide.com/e/e5940.html

[10] https://en.wikipedia.org/wiki/Ryokan_(inn)

[11] https://www.haikudesigns.com/tatami-mats.htm

[12] https://en.wikipedia.org/wiki/Vacuum_coffee_maker

[13] http://www.hida.jp/English/activities/sightseeing-information/

hirayu-grand-waterfall

[14] https://www.japan-guide.com/e/e2029_dress.html

[15] http://www.cnn.com/travel/article/guide-to-kaiseki-cuisine/index .html

[16]   https://savorjapan.com/contents/more-to-savor/kaiseki-cuisine-japans-artful-culinary-tradition-explained/

[17] https://en.wikipedia.org/wiki/Kaiseki

8

Day 8: Kappabashi Bridge, 1200-Year-Old Ginkgo Tree, and Wagyu Beef Experience

First thing in the morning, I felt my husband shaking me to wake me up from one of the deepest sleeps I've ever had. I looked at my watch and it was only 6 in the morning. I rolled over to my other side in the hopes of falling asleep again, but he was persistent. He said we have an hour before breakfast to enjoy our private bath. I didn't want to go because I was worried that in the light of day it wouldn't look as good as it did at night. Also, outside it seemed so foggy and cold. I saw how excited my husband was, so reluctantly, I stepped out of bed.

As soon as we opened the door to the outdoor bath, my indecisiveness disappeared. It was so beautiful. The clear water looked so inviting with the hot steam rising from the surface. Behind the fence we could see a mountain surrounded by fog and a Sakura tree in full bloom. The bath was much warmer in the morning than it was at night. The experience was unbelievable. I wish I were there right now.

Private outdoor bath at Nakamurakan ryokan.

Refreshed, we went to the food hall for our breakfast. The breakfast was a mixed western and traditional Japanese kaiseki breakfast. There were hard-boiled eggs and a few continental breakfast items on the tables next to the wall, but there were also traditional items, like miso soup, Ganmodoki (tofu and vegetable fritter), and *Natto*. Natto is one of the most hated Japanese foods for tourists. Hate it or love it, you can't stay indifferent to it.

Natto is a dish made of fermented soybeans. It has a very pungent smell, a strong flavor, and a slimy texture. Although the exact origin of Natto isn't known, there are a few stories about it dating to almost a 1,000 years ago. One of these stories is about Minamoto no Yoshiie. One day, while he was on a battle campaign, there was an attack while he was boiling soybeans. The soybeans were packed in a hurry into straw bags and were left there for a few days. When the bags were opened, the soybeans had already been fermented. The soldiers ate the soybeans and surprisingly enjoyed the flavor[1].

Although the flavor of Natto can be debatable, the nutritional values cannot. In a single cup of Natto you can get 134% of the Manganese,

84% of the Iron, 50% of the Magnesium, and 38% of the Calcium you need per day[2].

After we finished our breakfast, we went to the lobby to claim our free coffee at the *Coffee Corner*. We received a freshly brewed coffee and sat on the sofa facing the window. Outside it was still gloomy, but it had a cold beauty to it. The Sakura trees were covered by a blanket of fog, and the mountains peaked through the clouds. The lobby was very quiet, and it was so lovely just to sit there drinking our coffee and looking at the town through the window.

Our plans for the 8th day of our trip included a bus ride to *Shinhotaka-ropeway*. Shinhotaka-ropeway is a 1-hour bus ride from Hirayu. The ropeway offers over 1 km climb up the Hotake mountain and a magnificent view of the Okuhida region[3]. On the way up the mountain there is a stop where people can go to the visitor center, hiking trails, or even a public bath. At the highest point there is a restaurant, gift shop, and an observation deck. Usually, the mountains aren't covered in snow from late June to September.

Before going to the bus stop to catch a bus to Shinhotaka-ropeway, we decided to ask the receptionist if there is fog there. The clerk switched the channel on the TV to show a real-time view of Shinhotaka-ropeway. It looked even foggier than Hirayu. We decided not to go there because we wouldn't be able to enjoy the view. We asked the clerk if there is a different place we could go even though it's foggy. He suggested Kappabashi Bridge.

Tip: If you plan to visit Shinhotaka-ropeway, ask the reception clerk in your hotel whether there is fog there.

We went to the bus station to catch the bus to Kappabashi bridge. Before we purchased the ticket, we bought a Hida beef steamed bun from the vendor we missed the day before. To be honest, it had way more bun than meat. When we finished eating, my husband said he finally realized why the bun is usually filled with pork.

Left and Center: Breakfast at Nakamurakan ryokan. Right: Hida beef bun at Hirayu bus station.

A bus ticket to Kappabashi and back costs ¥4,100 per couple.

When we arrived, it was raining, but somehow it made the air fresher and the view better. We went to the trail that followed the banks of the Azusa river, and it led us towards the Kappabashi bridge. Although this bridge is an iconic symbol of Kamikochi, the bridge we saw was only 20 years old. The original bridge used to be a drawbridge, but in 1910 it was rebuilt to the first suspension bridge in Japan. The bridge, as well as its surroundings, offer a fantastic view of the Hotaka peaks and Mt. Myojindake[4].

The actual bridge isn't impressive at all, but if you know the story behind it, you can understand why it's such a popular tourist destination for Japanese people. In 1927, a novel named "Kappa" was written by Ryunosuke Akutagawa[5]. In this novel, a psychiatric patient accidentally arrives at the country filled with many Kappas (mythological creatures). Although the story is written about a fictitious culture, in reality, Akutagawa gives a satirical criticism of the Japanese culture during that time.

Fortunately for us, the rain and fog probably kept many of the tourists away from visiting the Kappa-bridge, so it wasn't crowded. We could enjoy the view of the snowy mountain hills and the river without looking at them through a crowd. The bridge itself, as well as the gift shop next to it, were actually crowded, but by no means at the scale of the golden week in Tokyo. Next to the bridge we saw a food stand that offers deep-fried pastries with different fillings. We bought a wasabi-filled pastry for ¥350. It was a perfectly comforting snack for this chilly weather.

Left: Mt. Myojindake. Right: deep-fried wasabi pastry.

We took the bus back to Hirayu. When we arrived, it was already lunchtime, and we went to explore the area around the hotel. We saw many small decorative fountains with onsen water. Some of them had a pot with eggs cooking inside. There were also many Sakura trees in full bloom. It is quite evident that the area is mostly tourist-oriented, but it is still very charming.

Left: cherry blossom. Right: eggs cooking in an onsen water-filled decorative fountain.

We went to *Yoshimoto* restaurant located next to Nakamurakan hotel. We ordered *Udon soup* and warm Soba noodles with shrimp tempura (for a total of ¥2,300 per couple). I liked the Soba noodles in Yoshimoto restaurant much more than the cold noodles we ate in Tokyo, but the star of the lunch was the Udon. Udon soup is soup with thick noodles made from wheat flour. Udon noodles are very popular in Japan and can also be served chilled with a dipping sauce[6]. The origin of Udon noodles isn't known, but it is believed it was brought to Japan from China during the Nara period[7].

Good to know: As was mentioned previously, slurping noodles is customary in Japan. However, slurping Udon noodles should be done with extra care, since they tend to spray broth if they are being slurped quickly.

The cool thing about the Udon soup in Yoshimoto restaurant was that it contained many wild vegetables grown in the mountains next to the restaurant. This soup gives you a new appreciation of local and seasonal foods. One wild vegetable I really liked was the *Yama Udo*. Yama Udo is mountain asparagus. It is a vegetable that grows in the mountains from early spring to late summer, but it can also be grown

108

in greenhouses[8]. I read a fun fact about Yama Udo: although it is considered a plant, it can grow up to about 2.5 meters.

Left: Udon soup. Right: Soba noodles soup at Yoshimoto restaurant.

We had about 30 minutes to wait for the bus to Takayama, so we decided to return to the foot onsen next to Nakamurakan hotel. It was so fun that we stayed there longer and caught the next bus. It's so great to visit this area of Japan during the time we were there. It wasn't too cold, but it was just cold enough to want to stick your feet (or body) into a warm bath. Besides, the area around the hotel felt so secluded. It was almost like we were the only tourists around. We had the foot onsen to ourselves, except for 15 minutes when a tourist lady joined us. In general, our stay in Hirayu offered a pleasant break from the crowd (but it might be because it was right after the golden week).

We went to the bus stop and purchased one-way tickets to Takayama for ¥3,240 per couple. It is actually the same bus we took when we came from Tokyo to Hirayu. The drive takes about one hour and offers many scenic views. The cool thing about taking the bus instead of the train is how close you get to rural homes on your way. Some of these rural houses have rice fields in their backyard.

The most productive way to grow rice in Japan is in a paddy field[9]. A paddy field is basically a flooded field with a thick layer of soft mud[10]. The reason why a paddy field is so effective in Japan is that Japan has suffered many volcanic eruptions that made the soil acidic. These conditions can promote rice growth in as little as a month[11]. Paddy farming has been used in Japan for about 2,000 years, but as rice consumption started to fall in recent years, many people are worried for the Japanese culture, since rice used to be the heart of it[12].

Country hotel (¥6,800 per room per night), the hotel we booked in Takayama, is located right across the street from Takayama Station. That was very convenient both when we arrived and when we left. After settling in the hotel, we went (you've guessed it) in search of food. On the way, we came by Hida Kokubunji Temple. This temple is a three-pagoda structure, and it's the oldest temple in Takayama, as it was reconstructed 500 years ago[13]. Kokubunji temple is a Buddhist temple, and it has a row of Buddhist statues on its premises.

Another great thing you can find on the temple grounds is a 1200-year-old Ginkgo tree. This Ginkgo tree has been designated as a natural national monument. The height of the Ginkgo tree is 28 meters, and its circumference is 10 meters. It was once believed that snow will start as soon as the Ginkgo tree starts to shed its leaves. Under the Ginkgo tree there is a Jizo statue.

Jizo is a merciful deity who helps people gain health and success and eases people's suffering[14]. In one of the numerous texts that describe Jizo, it is said that he will remain amongst us to help souls fight against hell's torments. In modern Japan, people believe Jizo is also the guardian of all unborn babies. This belief is unique to Japan and isn't prevalent in other parts of Asia. He is also believed to help mothers obtain better milk for nursing[15]. Nowadays, Japanese people consider Jizo to be one of the most beloved deities who is a friend to both adults and children. They believe Jizo will help them without conditions in their time of need, either during their lives or deaths.

After visiting the temple, we entered a small shop that sells sake. There, we bought a sake the salesman suggested, since we are not very educated in sake. Takayama has many sake breweries, and the sake produced there are considered some of the best in Japan[16]. Some people travel to Takayama for a sake tour during mid-January to late February when a few of the breweries open their doors to the public.

Our first gastronomic stop this evening was an Izakaya located 15 minutes walk from our hotel. We were seated on floor cushions at the back of the Izakaya where we had complete privacy. The place was very nice and more spacious than it seemed from the outside. We ordered 3 breaded skewers, a few tempura items (including white fish and shrimp), and *Okonomiyaki.*

Okonomiyaki is a pan-fried pancake made of batter, cabbage, and a variation of additional ingredients and toppings[17]. Okonomiyaki is available in all its different varieties throughout Japan, but it's most popular in the western parts of Japan. Some food researchers believe the first variation of Okonomiyaki dates back to the 16th century[18], but prior to the 1920s it was a thin sweet crepe. During the 20s, savory crepe varieties started to appear. During WWII, there was a shortage of rice, so savory crepes with readily available ingredients became a favorite food.

Okonomiyaki was one of the Japanese dishes I had read about before coming to Japan. As soon as I saw a picture of it or a video of people eating it on YouTube, I knew it was a dish I had to try. Not only do I like cabbage and fried batter, but the added sauce, mayonnaise stripes, and the bonito flakes (dried tuna) give the dish a magnificently appealing look. We ordered one Okonomiyaki for the four of us, and I'm glad we did. It is definitely a dish worth trying, but it is very filling. It didn't reach my list of the best meals I ate in Japan, but I'm glad I tried it.

The interesting thing about the restaurant was that they had a Call Button. A call button is used to summon the waiter. It can be handy, especially when your table isn't in the waiter's field of view.

Since we are in the Hida region, and Hida is part of the area where Wagyu beef comes from, our next food stop was obvious for us. We went to *Tenaga Ashinaga Hommachi* restaurant to finally try Wagyu beef. Wagyu beef is a type of beef cattle that originated in Japan. Wagyu literally means Japanese ('Wa') cow ('gyu')[19]. Compared to regular beef, Wagyu beef has more fat inside their muscles. Therefore, they have higher physical endurance than other types of beef, so they were initially used for agriculture.

Although the Wagyu genetic strain was found to be separated approximately 35,000 years ago, the modern Wagyu beef is a result of crossing Japanese breeds with imported breeds about 150 years ago[20]. Back then, the Japanese government wanted to introduce western food to Japan, so the Wagyu beef was genetically modified, so it could be consumed. The intramuscular fat provides the meat a marbled look and great texture. The marbling gives the meat a unique flavor and tenderness that is impossible to get from another breed of beef.

The way Wagyu beef is raised is very unique. First, grazing is very uncommon, so the cattle mostly spend their entire lives in the barn[21]. Second, they get a bottle of beer a day when they lose their appetites due to summer heat. Lastly, to increase their marbling the Wagyu cattle get a daily massage, sometimes with Sake[22].

Good to know: Wagyu beef sometimes carries the name of the region it was raised in. Hida beef, Kobe beef, Matsusaka beef, Yonezawa beef, Mishima beef, and Omi beef are all types of Wagyu beef[23].

Each piece of Wagyu beef produced in Japan has a tracking record that includes the bloodline information of the cattle and information on the way it was raised. Restaurants can provide you with the tracking number of the piece you order, and you can find all the information about the cattle in the National Livestock Breeding Center (NLBC) website. Moreover, each piece is categorized with a specific grade based on its yield (A-C, where A is considered the best yield), and overall quality (1-5, where 5 is the highest quality)[24].

My husband and I ordered a 120g steak of A5 Hida beef sirloin to share and two glasses of Japanese red wine (for a total of ¥4,850). First, we got the wine which was very light with a hint of sweetness. After a few minutes, the steaming wagyu beef arrived. Straight away, the most appetizing smell surrounded us. The sirloin steak was cut into bite-size pieces and was served with two accompanying sauces and some Himalayan salt. Next to the steak was a small pile of fried garlic. The steak was absolutely fantastic. It didn't taste like any piece of meat I've ever had. It was so juicy and soft that I can't remember actually chewing it. It felt like it melted in my mouth. I didn't want to dilute the taste with any of the sauces, but I did add a piece of garlic, and it was divine.

Left: Okonomiyaki. Right: Hida beef steak atTenaga Ashinaga Hommachi restaurant.

We just finished enjoying our fantastic steak, when the chef of the restaurant came to greet us. He asked where we were from, and we thanked him for the most unbelievable steak.

Sources:

[1] https://en.wikipedia.org/wiki/Natt%C5%8D

[2] https://draxe.com/natto/

[3] https://www.japan-guide.com/e/e5943.html

[4] http://www.kamikochi.org/spot/kappa-bridge

[5] https://en.wikipedia.org/wiki/Kappa_(novel)

[6] https://www.japan-talk.com/jt/new/japanese-food-list

[7] http://web-japan.org/kidsweb/cook/soba/soba01.html

[8] http://www.specialtyproduce.com/produce/Yama_Udo_10065.php

[9] https://en.wikipedia.org/wiki/Paddy_field

[10] http://imaginatorium.org/sano/tanbo.htm

[11] https://en.wikipedia.org/wiki/Paddy_field

[12] https://www.japantimes.co.jp/life/2016/01/29/food/the-future-of-rice-farming-in-japan/#.Wix5qUqnFPY

[13] http://www.hida.jp/English/activities/sightseeing-information/nara-period-state-supported-temples

[14] http://www.onmarkproductions.com/html/jizo1.shtml

[15] http://kazekaolboy98.holy.jp/the-kokubunnji-temple/

[16] https://samuraitrip.com/en/takayama/articles/sake-breweries-takayama

[17] https://www.japan-guide.com/r/e100.html

[18] https://en.wikipedia.org/wiki/Okonomiyaki

[19] http://wagyu.org/breed-info/what-is-wagyu/

[20] http://wagyu.org/breed-info/what-is-wagyu/

[21] http://www.luciesfarm.com/artman/publish/article_39.php

[22] https://notesofnomads.com/kobe-beef/

[23] https://en.wikipedia.org/wiki/Wagyu

[24] http://edition.cnn.com/travel/article/cnngo-japan-beef-wagyu/index.html

9

Day 9: Morning Market, Hida Folk Village, Wagyu Beef Sushi, and Beef Bowls

First thing this morning, we took a walk towards the morning market. While walking in the streets of Takayama, it's very hard not to notice a small red doll everywhere you look. This faceless red doll is called *Sarubobo*, which literally means a monkey baby[1]. A sarubobo is a charm that brings good fortune. The sarubobo is usually red because monkey babies have a red face, and because the color red is believed to protect against evil[2]. However, Sarubobo can also come in other colors, such as yellow, gold, pink, green, purple, and black. Each color is said to give good fortune in a different field of life. For example, pink brings good fortune in love, while yellow provides good luck in gambling[3].

Today, a Sarubobo doll is one of the most famous souvenirs in Japan, but its origin dates back to the Nara period (about 1200 years ago). Back then, the Sarubobo doll was brought from China. In that period, the Sarubobo was the only toy available for girls. Over time the doll's appearance has changed (mostly color).

According to a sign I saw in Takayama, each Sarubobo doll is handmade. For people who are interested in learning how to make their own Sarubobo doll instead of buying it, there is a class in Takayama that teaches how to make Sarubobo dolls by hand[3].

It is not surprising that there is a class that teaches people how to make Sarubobo dolls in Takayama, since the doll is originally from Hida region. Japan has many souvenirs or food items that are available for purchase only in the particular prefectures where they originate. However, for people who are staying in Tokyo and still want to purchase souvenirs from different prefectures, the local governments offer a great option. This option is called "Antenna Shops."[4] These shops were first established during the 90s as a way to promote local products and ingredients to the nation's capital[5]. Today they offer a wide variety of regional specialty food items, souvenirs, unique drinks, and spices from different prefectures.

The morning market in Takayama is one of the largest morning markets in Japan[6]. It has many stalls with Sarubobo souvenirs and a few food stalls. We tried the Hida beef bun which was too sweet for me, and we got 10 fish-shaped pastries for the four of us (for ¥500). The pastries came with a variety of stuffing, including green tea, custard, and my favorite: red beans. We also stumbled upon a miso shop that sells miso produced in a factory not far from the market. The shop provides tastings of the delicious different miso on sale. As was mentioned earlier, miso is fermented soybeans. It has long been a staple food in the Japanese kitchen and is the main ingredient of miso soup. Miso consists of cooked soybeans combined with rice, barley or rye, and a mold culture (koji)[7]. The color and flavor of the miso highly depend on the ingredient amounts and fermentation time. Longer fermentation times (three years) produce miso with a richer flavor.

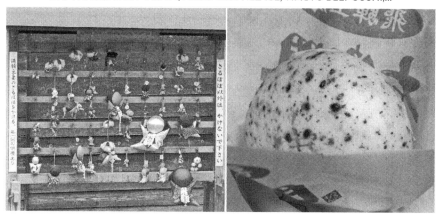

Left: Sarubobo doll. Right: Hida beef bun.

While today the Takayama market mainly offers souvenirs, 300 years ago, when the market was originated, it primarily sold mulberry tree leaves to feed silkworms. Silk originated in China about 8,500 years ago[8]. The production of silk in Japan was adopted from China and Korea during the 3rd century. Since then, the Japanese refined the silk production technique, and today the Japanese silk is considered to be of very high quality[9]. It is used for traditional garments, scarfs, and art.

From the Morning market, we continued to Takayama Station and purchased a round-trip ticket to Hida folk village (for ¥930 per person). We arrived at the folk village at 9AM and paid the entrance fee (¥700 per person). At this time, the village was almost entirely empty. As time passed, it started to fill with tourists and school students.

Good to know: Hida folk village is open every day between 8:30AM to 5PM.

Hida folk village is an open-air museum founded in 1971. The museum has an exhibit of more than 30 different types of traditional buildings relocated from different parts of the Hida region[10]. The traditional structures were placed around the Goami pond, which was built at the beginning of the 1930s to supply water to the nearby rice fields. The 100-500-year-old buildings and the beautiful pond convey the look of a picturesque village.

Hida folk village.

The building styles of the various houses in the folk village are very unique. For instance, some of the buildings have an earthen floor, *tataki*. Tataki is made out of a mixture of red clay, lime, salt, and water. This floor keeps a constant humidity level in the house and doesn't let dust rise from it. The roofs in the village are also unique. Many of the buildings have a shingled roof. The shingled roofs were made from thin pieces of chestnut wood, weighed down by large stones. The chestnut wood was chosen since it doesn't easily rot. The shingled roof can protect against rain and snow for 30 years.

Inside the buildings, you can find information about the silk production in the Hida region. The Hida region had a limited soil for farming, so the silk production became the primary source of income in the area. As a result of the wide range of temperatures between day and night, the silk produced in this area was of very high quality.

Besides the traditional buildings, there are six status of Jizo that surround the pond. These statues date back to 1740 when they were placed at a crematory in Takayama-shi Soyuji-cho. The statues were placed there to pray for the souls of the dead, since they are believed to represent the six realms of existence. In Buddhism, the six realms of existence represent the six phases of the endless cycle of birth, life, and death[11].

We went back to the bus station to catch the bus back to Takayama station when we noticed a beautiful Japanese maple tree. Turns out there is a type of maple that is very common in Japan called Kaede. The Japanese maple isn't restricted to Japan and can also be found across Korea and in some areas in China, Russia, and Mongolia[12]. During the Fall months, the Japanese people have a tradition to go and view the maple trees as they change their colors into shades of yellow, orange, and red. This tradition is called *Momiji-gari*. For Shinto believers, Momiji-gari is a way to communicate with nature and the spirits.

When we exited the bus, we went to search for something to eat in Takayama old town. We looked for a restaurant that serves eel since we only tried it once this trip. During our search, we came across a long line of school kids on their way home from school. Many of them stood in line next to a window in the wall. When we came closer, we realized you can order take out Hida beef sushi through the window.

The establishment is located in Kotte gyu in the old town of Takayama. There are only four different menu sets available, but each selection is terrific. My husband and I got two sets to share. The first set consisted of two lightly seared Hida beef nigiri, and one seared Hida beef gunkan (a type of sushi) with a quail egg yolk on top. The second consisted of two raw Hida beef nigiri. The unexpected part was that the sets were served on a prawn rice cracker. This way, when you are done enjoying the sushi, you can eat the plate as a dessert.

I enjoyed both kinds of the Hida beef nigiri, but the absolute highlight was the gunkan. The mixture of tastes and textures in this one tiny bite were unbelievable. I was only sorry that my husband didn't try it. You can purchase Hida beef nigiri in Kotte gyu in the old town of Takayama every day between 9AM and 5PM (cash only).

Left: Hida beef sushi served on a rice cracker. Right: a Japanese maple tree.

After the small appetizers, we continued our search for a place to eat in the old town. Takayama old town is a charming place to take a walk. It has many shops, houses, and even sake breweries that are a few centuries old[13]. However, we were too preoccupied with finding the best place for lunch. Finally, we stumbled upon *Unashin* restaurant that serves eel, which is located a couple of minutes away from the Hida beef sushi. We arrived during lunch, so we ordered two set eel meals. Both meals consisted of an eel with rice, but one of them was topped with seaweed and eggs. Both meals came with a bowl of soup, *Hiyayakko* (cold tofu), and some pickles. Each meal was served on a tray in traditional tableware. It is so satisfying to receive your food in such a lovely detail-oriented manner. It is true what they say, people do eat with their eyes first. Just by taking in this lovely image in front of me, I was already starting to feel satisfied.

Admittedly, I don't like eel. Back home, whenever we go to a sushi restaurant I try to steer clear of any menu item that contains eel in it. That being said, when we arrived in Japan, I decided to give eel a chance. What better place to do it than in a restaurant devoted to eel? Indeed, my choice didn't disappoint. The eel was full of flavors and cooked to perfection. While it is still not my favorite food, I am willing to eat it again at this restaurant.

Left: traditional tableware. Right: an eel meal at Unashin restaurant.

Sadly, our time in Takayama came to an end. I enjoyed our time in Takayama, and I believe that if our trip were longer, we would have spent more time there. My husband and I gathered our things and went to Takayama Station to catch a bus to Kyoto. It was still a little early, so first we went to have some coffee in the information café at the station. Meanwhile, our friends went to a convenience store to get some shopping done.

The information café wasn't busy during these after lunch hours. We ordered coffees to go, and we sat at a table to wait for the bus. While we were waiting for the coffees, one of the workers started drawing a geisha on the blackboard. Although the café is located in the bus station, it has a very charming and youthful atmosphere. We got our coffees, and we noticed the cups also had a drawing on them. That was so nice! What a friendly staff.

Information cafe at Takayama station.

Our friends rejoined us a few minutes before the bus arrived. Similarly to our bus drive from Tokyo to Hirayu, we booked this bus in advance. The trip is also around 4 hours long and passes through rural parts of the country. On the way to Kyoto, we passed by Lake Biwa. Lake Biwa is the largest freshwater lake in Japan[14]. What is most interesting about this lake is its age. Lake Biwa is at least 4 million years old and is one of the oldest lakes in the world. Due to this impressive age, this lake is habitat to at least a thousand different species and subspecies.

We had a 15 minutes stop on the way. I ran to the washroom because I saw a bus full of female gymnasts arriving before us, and I was worried the bus would leave without me if I'm late. When I got to the washroom, I saw the longest line of young Japanese girls in front of me. The line was so long that it proceeded way outside the washroom. I decided to wait in line. To my great surprise, the line was moving very fast. I soon approached the entrance to the washroom. Finally, it dawned on me. On the wall right in front of the entrance, there was an electronic plan of the washroom giving real-time information of all the occupied and free stalls. Also, the girls weren't taking their time, so there was a constant stream of girls going in and out of the stalls. If I didn't want to use the washroom, I would have spent some time just observing this Japanese efficiency at its finest. Needless to say, I walked out of the restroom with a lot of time to spare.

I located my husband, and we went to get a snack for the rest of the road trip. Inside the station we found a food vendor that sells a bunch of deep-fried pastries, dried fish, and sausages. We got a deep-fried pastry and a sausage on a stick. We also had some extremely spicy wasabi rice crackers with us (that we bought a few days earlier in a convenience store).

Left: deep-fried pastries, dried fish, and sausages inside a bus station on the way to Kyoto. Right: an electronic sign giving real-time information of a washroom at a bus station.

We arrived in Kyoto, and we went to the hostel we booked. New Piece hostel (about ¥10,200 per night per room) is located very close to Kawaramachi Station. The location is great since it is within walking distance of many shops and from the Nishiki market. This hostel has modern private rooms in addition to shared rooms. However, the room we stayed in was the smallest one we had so far. There wasn't enough space to open our suitcase. Still, this stay was one of our favorite hotels during the trip. Not only that breakfast was included in the price, but the lobby also had computers the guests could use. We used a computer to upload our images from the memory card to Google Drive. Moreover, the hostel staff was very helpful and friendly.

After we managed to open our suitcases, we went to explore the area. We headed towards Teramachi street. Teramachi street is one of the most famous streets in Kyoto[15]. Today, it is mostly known for its excellent selection of art galleries and clothing shops, but this street has more than 400 years of history. In 1590, during the great reconstruction of Kyoto, many temples from various locations across Kyoto were relocated to the east side of Higashi Kyogoku Oji street. Following the relocation of the temples into this street, its name was changed to Teramachi, which literally means "temple street." Later, many shops specializing in spiritual goods started to appear across the street.

In Teramachi street we went to the Red Rock restaurant. We ordered the roast beef bowl and the steak bowl, which are two of their most popular dishes. We weren't prepared for what came next. We received two big bowls filled with rice with a mountain of meat sitting on top. The meat in the steak bowl is raw, topped with a raw egg yolk and yogurt. Both dishes were great. The combination of the yogurt and egg yolk with the meat tasted terrific. The rice was great as well. Overall it was a very affordable (¥1,730 per couple) and delicious meal.

After the amazing meal, we walked around Teramachi street until we finally arrived at a restaurant located under Agu hair lex. Here we ordered an Okonomiyaki (¥880). We got two orders for the four of us, since we were mostly full after the huge meat bowls. The pre-made Okonomiyaki was placed on a hot plate in the middle of the table, and an egg yolk was placed in the center of the green onions topping. I was a bit disappointed because when I saw the hot plate in the middle of the table, I was hoping the Okonomiyaki would be made from scratch in front of us. Nevertheless, the taste wasn't affected by my slight disappointment. However, ordering an Okonomiyaki right after the meal in the Red Rock wasn't the best idea. The Okonomiyaki is a very filling dish, and it tastes much better on an empty stomach. When we finished eating, we rolled back to our rooms for a highly needed night's sleep.

Left and Top Right: steak and beef bowls at Red Rock restaurant. Bottom Right: Okonomiyaki .

Sources:
[1] http://jpninfo.com/20110

[2] https://japanwalkersea.com/takayama-japanese-doll-sarubobo/

[3] http://jpninfo.com/20110

[4] https://travel.gaijinpot.com/yurakucho-ginza-antenna-shops/

[5] https://en.japantravel.com/tokyo/antenna-shops-in-tokyo/27109

[6] http://www.hida.jp/English/activities/sightseeing-information

/morning-market

[7] https://permaculturenews.org/2012/02/04/making-miso/

[8] https://en.wikipedia.org/wiki/Silk

[9] https://en.wikipedia.org/wiki/Japanese_silk

[10] https://www.japan-guide.com/e/e5901.html

[11] https://en.wikipedia.org/wiki/Sa%E1%B9%83s%C4%81ra_(Buddhism)

[12] https://dengarden.com/landscaping/japanese-maple-trees

[13] https://www.japan-guide.com/e/e5903.html

[14] https://en.wikipedia.org/wiki/Lake_Biwa

[15] http://thekyotoproject.org/English/teramachi-dori-teramachi-street/

10

Day 10: Torii Trail, Japanese Knives, Ancient Temple, and Shopping

We woke up early and took the subway to Fushimi Inari-Taisha shrine. We wanted to arrive as early as possible, since this shrine is a very famous tourist attraction, and we tried to avoid the crowd as much as possible. It's not a wonder this shrine is so crowded. Not only is this shrine absolutely beautiful with over 1,200 years of history, but it is also the most important shrine dedicated to *Inari*. Inari is the Shinto god of rice[1]. Close to the shrine there are many fox statues, since a fox is said to be Inari's messenger.

Good to know: Fushimi Inari-Taisha shrine (torii trail in Kyoto) becomes very crowded starting from 10AM each day. The peak hours are 10AM-4PM during Saturday and Sunday.

On the way leading to the shrine, we got deep-fried cheese sticks from a food vendor. It's so great that food is so readily available even next to shrines and temples. When we arrived at Fushimi Inari-Taisha shrine, there were already many tourists there, but it wasn't too crowded. We had enough room to enjoy the vibrant color of the shrine and its beautiful structure.

Good to know: Although many shrines and temples have food vendors and stalls on their grounds, it is considered highly disrespectful to eat on the grounds away from the food stalls[2].

Left: Fushimi Inari-Taisha. Right: deep-fried cheese sticks.

For many tourists, however, the main attraction isn't the shrine itself. Behind the main buildings of Fushimi Inari-Taisha shrine, there are many wooded trails leading to the top of Mount Inari. The trails are shadowed by thousands of parallel Torii gates called *Senbon Torii*. Each gate was donated to the shrine by companies or individuals. The cost varies between ¥400,000 to over ¥1,000,000, depending on the size of the gates.

While we were walking through the trail of Torii gates, we overheard a tour guide telling his group the Torii gates are supposed to bring good luck to the person who donates it. One of the group members asked: "does this mean that people who donate the big gates will have more luck?". To which the guide answered: "No, it just means they have more money."

Torii gate trail next to Fushimi Inari-Taisha shrine.

It is very challenging to explain in words how spectacular this place is. Imagine you are walking in a long network of bright red bridges. Each bridge is its own masterpiece with beautifully written Japanese names on its back side. In between the gates, you are getting splashes of sun rays from the top and flashing images of a shaded forest filled with fresh bright green leaves from the sides.

We didn't proceed to the top because the entire hike up and down the trail takes approximately 3 hours. When we left the shrine, we passed through the street food vendors again. We bought a chicken and leek skewer from one of the vendors. I can easily say it was the best Yakitori we had in Japan. It was so juicy and perfectly cooked. This just goes to show that you can never tell where the best food in Japan is going to be. It can come from a high-end restaurant, small Izakaya, or even a food vendor next to a shrine.

It was a warm day, which became very apparent to us after leaving the shaded forest. Each moment that passed brought with it an increase in temperature. It was starting to be unbearable to stand in the sun, but the street didn't offer much shade. Luckily, we found the best solution possible. We located a shop that sells *Kakigōri*.

Kakigōri is a Japanese dessert that consists of shaved ice topped with a sweet syrup and sometimes condensed milk. The Kakigōri dates back at least to the Heian period (~11th century). During that time, the naturally formed ice (during cold winters) was shaved with a knife into a bowl and served with a variety of saps and syrups[3]. It used to be considered a very luxurious dessert that was only available to nobility. During the late 19th century there was a revolution in ice availability in Japan when Kahe Nakagawa invented an ice maker. Up to this point Japan used to import ice from the US. The new ice maker, along with the invention of an ice shaving machine, led to the commercially available Kakigōri.

We purchased a strawberry flavored Kakigōri for ¥400. It definitely helped to cope with the heat but didn't help us with our thirst. We finished our water bottle during our hike in the Torii trails. Luckily, we were in Japan where a vending machine is never too far away. The availability of the vending machines is really something to admire. We never had to carry more than a small plastic bottle of water wherever we went.

The same cannot be said about garbage bins. Locating a public garbage bin in Japan is almost impossible, but it wasn't like this before 1995. In 1995 there was a deadly terror attack in the subway trains in Tokyo where five cult members released deadly sarin gas[4]. As a way to prevent future terror attacks, the government removed garbage bins from the streets.

Tip: It's recommended that you carry a bag with you wherever you go to avoid situations where you have something you need to dispose of but can't find a garbage bin around.

Good to know: Most of the places that offer you items that will later need disposal also have a garbage bin. Some examples include vending machines, convenience stores, or even food vendors.

We went back to the subway station where we purchased an *Inarizushi* filled with eel. An Inarizushi is a deep-fried tofu in a pocket shape filled with rice[5]. It's not surprising to find Inarizushi near the Fushimi Inari-Taisha shrine since both are dedicated to Inari. According to Japanese folklore, the deep-fried tofu is also the favorite food of Inari's fox messengers. Maybe I have some fox blood in me because I also loved this pocket filled with goodness. Not only was the *Inarizushi* absolutely tasty but it also looked like a tiny piece of art.

Top Left: Inarizushi. Bottom Left: chicken and leek Yakitori. Right: Kakigori.

We took the subway to Gion-Shijo station and walked towards Hayakawa Hamonoten knife shop. We chose this place to purchase a knife not only because it offers a unique experience, great variety, superb quality, and helpful staff, but it also offers affordable prices. When we entered, the store was empty, and we were greeted by a friendly person named Kenji.

We looked through the shop's collection not knowing what to get. Both my husband and I love cooking, so each of us wanted our own knife. Kenji helped us choose the right knife for each of us. He was very patient and explained the difference in size, shape, use of each knife, and metal composition. Different metal compositions rust at a different rate, so we chose rust-resistant knives.

Tip: If you plan to purchase a knife in Japan, I suggest doing some research online, so you can pick the knife that best suits your needs.

When we selected our knives, Kenji asked if there was anything we wanted to engrave on it (with no extra charge). We decided to engrave our initials. He handed us a piece of paper and we wrote our initials in English. He translated it into Japanese and wrote it on the same piece of paper. Then, he went to the back of the store to call his father-in-law, Masaya. Masaya greeted us and looked at the knives we selected. He told us he's been working in this store for the past 70 years. He also explained about these knives and said that with proper care they can be used for up to 50 years. Then he took out a knife from under the counter and told us his wife used this knife for 41 years. With each sharpening, the knife's blade became smaller, and the knife he showed us was indeed much narrower than the knives we selected.

Tip: When buying a knife in Japan, it is worth investing in a rust-resistant knife, since it is easiest to take care of. Simply wash and dry the knife after use, and it can last you for many years.

Masaya then took Kenji's note and our knife for engraving. I was a bit worried at this point. Masaya's hands were shaking when he talked to us. After all, he must be at least 85 years old. Nevertheless, as soon as he touched the knife, his hands stopped shaking. It was quite astonishing. Each one of his movements was extraordinarily precise. When he finished, I looked at the engraving and the note side by side.

To me, they look identical.

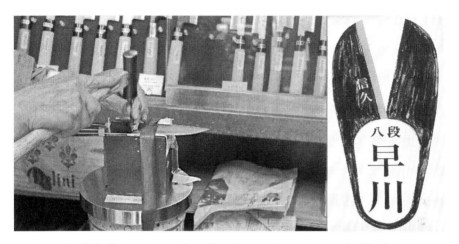

A knife being engraved at Hayakawa Hamonoten knife shop.

My astonishment didn't end there. Next thing I knew, Masaya told my husband to follow him to the sharpening station where he taught him how to correctly sharpen the knives. The tutorial took much longer than the time it took us to select the knives. Masaya explained each movement in detail and also showed precisely what not to do. Masaya doesn't speak English, but he knows all the essential words for someone to completely understand him. I'm not sure how long the lesson actually was, but I estimate it took 15-20 minutes. We added a sharpening stone to our purchase, so we can adequately sharpen the knives. The total for both knives and sharpening stone was about ¥27,000. When we finished our shopping, the same process began for our friends. Both Masaya and Kenji give 100% of their focus to each customer.

Knives in Japan are considered the highest quality in the world. The quality of the knives reflects their cultural importance. During ancient times, it was believed that a *samurai*'s sword was his soul[6]. As time passed, the art of sword making was replaced by the art of knife making, but the main techniques and fabrication skills have been passed from one generation to the next to keep the same characteristics of the traditional swords. In fact, the production process of a kitchen knife is so similar to the production process of a traditional sword that the city that was once the center of sword production in Japan (Seki[7]) is now the center of kitchen knife production. Although knife production replaced the sword production in Japan, one can still claim the knife is the soul of a chef, like the sword is the soul of a *samurai*.

A samurai is an ancient Japanese warrior. During the Heian period (794-1185), wealthy landowners grew independent of the government[8]. They hired samurai to make an army for their own protection. During the late 12th century, two independent landowner clans battled to gain control over the country. Minamoto Yoritomo clan won the war and gained dominance over Japan for the next 700 years. During this time, they established a new dictatorship military government with a shogun (military commander) at its head. The samurai enforced the authority of the shogun, which increased his power over the emperor[9]. Starting from the early 17th century, there were 250 years of peace in Japan. During this time, the samurai began taking up trading or government positions. The samurai began to adopt the principle of Buddhism, and it became the predominant religion of the samurai.

This entire experience at the knife shop made me think about how old age and experience is revered in Japan. I am sure Kenji would have done fantastic work, similar to Masaya. However, he called Masaya, who is more experienced. We encountered this behavior in many places during our stay in Japan. Each time we went to a coffee shop, our order was taken by someone that hurried to the back of the shop to call the more senior person to make the coffee for us. Not only that, but Japan has an annual Respect for the Aged Day[10]. The Respect for the Aged Day is a designated Japanese holiday to honor the senior citizens. On this day, the Japanese media features the oldest people in the country.

Before we left the knife store, we talked with Kenji about the different foods we love in Japan. When we said we love Ramen, his eyes lit up. He said this is one of his favorite foods. We asked him to recommend a good Ramen place, and he recommended a restaurant located 10 minutes away from the shop. After we thanked both Masaya and Kenji, we headed towards the restaurant (located under Irish Pub Field). There, we ordered pork Ramen and curry Ramen (for ¥1,750). It wasn't the best Ramen we had, but definitely not the worst.

Left: curry Ramen. Right: pork Ramen.

After lunch, we took the subway to Kiyomizudera temple. Kiyomizud-era temple appears on the UNESCO World Heritage List as a historical monument of ancient Kyoto. The temple was built in the late 700s next to the Otowa Waterfall, but the buildings that can be seen today only date back to 1633[11]. The temple is named after the pure water of the waterfall[12]. In the main hall, there is a small statue of Kannon, the goddess of mercy. Next to the main hall there is a wooden veranda that allows a great view of the hillside below. Interestingly, the main hall and the wooden veranda were built without the use of nails.

Good to know: Kiyomizudera temple requires a significant hike up many stairs.

Good to know: The water from the falls next to Kiyomizudera temple is said to have therapeutic powers. It's said that if a person drinks water from the three streams of the waterfall, he will have better health, longevity, and success in studies[13].

Behind the main hall stands a Jishu shrine dedicated to the deity of love and matchmaking. Outside of the shrine there are two stones 18 meters apart. It is believed that if a person can find his way from one stone to the next with his eyes closed, he will find love.

Tip: If you are visiting Kiyomizudera temple with your significant other, the veranda offers a very romantic spot to look at the sunset.

When we came to the temple, there were many renovations and reconstructions in the area, so the wooden stage was closed to visitors. We just walked around the site and enjoyed the view.

We climbed all the stairs back down and headed towards the Hello Kitty café. Unfortunately, the café closed at 5PM, and we were too late. The shop next to the café was still open when we came, so we got us some cute Hello Kitty souvenirs.

Hello Kitty was created by Sanrio company in 1975. As of 2014, Hello Kitty brand generates $7 billion a year[14]. Interestingly, although Hello Kitty is loved by many, some use her as a type of punishment. In a precinct in Thailand, the officers that break the rules need to wear a bright pink Hello Kitty armband as punishment[15].

The surrounding area to the Kiyomizudera temple is filled with shops and old structures. There are also many people walking around dressed in traditional Japanese clothes. We enjoyed our walk, but besides buying some souvenirs in the Hello Kitty shop, we didn't purchase anything else. We were looking for teacups, but we couldn't find anything we liked, especially since many of the stores offered the same products.

My husband and our friend did find something they liked, but it wasn't a teacup. They found a place that sells ice cream with soy sauce! When they joined us ladies with their new purchase, they told us it was the best ice cream they have ever had. They said the combination of ice cream and soy sauce was amazing. We believed them and tried some as well. I am sorry, but ice cream and soy sauce DO NOT MIX. I didn't like it at all. To my great surprise, my husband and our friend didn't prank us. They actually enjoyed the combination of tastes. To each his own, I guess. To those of you who want to try this new flavor combination, it cost only ¥380.

Left: women in traditional clothes. Center: Kiyomizudera temple. Right: ice cream with soy sauce.

According to our plan, our next destination was Pontocho alley. This alley is said to be one of the dining areas with the best ambiance in Kyoto[16]. Many restaurants in the alley offer dishes ranging from traditional Kyoto to modern Kyoto, and foreign cuisine. When we arrived at the alley, we immediately had a flashback to the tourist trap we visited in Tokyo (Golden Gai). Most of the restaurants we passed by in Pontocho alley were relatively expensive and charged table fees (especially the restaurants that offer a view of Kamogawa River).

Another reason why Pontocho alley is such a tourist destination (other than the river view) is its location. The alley is only a short walk away from Gion district. In Gion district, there are many old structures, teahouses, and it is not uncommon to see a *geisha* or *maiko* walk in the street[17]. A geisha is a high-class female entertainer who is trained in various art forms[18], whereas a maiko is an apprentice geisha. Their skills include the art of conversation, entertaining guests, dancing, and playing musical instruments[19].

The history of the geisha dates back to the 16th century when the shogun designated quarters in which prostitution was legally allowed[20]. As time passed, these quarters became popular not only for sex, but also for entertainment. Some of the courtesans in these quarters were entertaining with music, dancing, or even calligraphy. At the end of the 17th century the first geishas appeared, but unlike today, the first geishas were male. In the 1750s the first female geisha appeared. She was a very talented singer, as well as a courtesan, and she became extremely popular. Following her success, many female geishas started to appear and perform as entertainers only, and not as courtesans (who were still popular).

We decided to leave Pontocho alley and find a restaurant that doesn't charge a table fee. Two minutes away from Pontocho alley we came across a German restaurant named Munchen restaurant. The restaurant displayed plastic replicas of its food and beer menu in the display window. The big beautiful meals, great variety, and giant beer cups attracted us, and we entered.

The restaurant was mostly full and the atmosphere was cheerful. When we received the menu, we had a difficult time deciding what we wanted to get. There were so many options, and they all looked so good. We knew we want a beer and something that would agree with the beer. While we were struggling to pick things from the menu, we suddenly observed there was a picture on the wall right above our table. The picture featured three perfectly round, golden-brown, deep-fried crab balls dipped in a shallow tomato dip. As soon as we saw this picture, it was clear this was going to be our first choice. We also ordered carpaccio and an omelet (the specialty of the restaurant). Everything was very good, but I especially enjoyed the crab balls. We were delighted with the choice of restaurant and with the price of the meal (¥3,430 per couple without any table fees).

After the restaurant, we headed towards the hostel. On our way, we entered a cool shop called "Loft." Loft is a chain store that sells everyday items and household goods. The store has many levels, each more interesting than the previous one. While we were looking for a few office supplies, we also enjoyed scanning the store for cool items for the kitchen. We lost track of time, and before we realized, the store was closing. We hurried to the cashier to pay for our items. What impressed us most was that the cashier used a special bag for pens. It was the smallest bag we've ever seen. What a wonderfully detail-oriented country!

Last stop before we called it a night was a little ice cream street stand close to the hostel. The stand also sells fish-shaped pastries. My husband and I got one of each and went to our tiny room for a long-anticipated rest.

Left: crab balls. Center: Japanese omelet at Munchen restaurant. Right: fish-shaped pastry.

Sources:

[1] https://www.japan-guide.com/e/e3915.html

[2] https://www.japan-guide.com/forum/quereadisplay.html?0+105464

[3] http://www.inhamamatsu.com/recommend/cat2/7/japans-kakigori.php

[4] http://jpninfo.com/54373

[5] https://gurunavi.com/en/japanfoodie/2017/10/a-guide-to-inarizushi-japans-sweet-sushi-tofu-pockets.html?__ngt__=TT0df 24d0c7001ac1e4ae862GzRwn43IRrpDnj75veGfdf

[6] https://www.echefknife.com/a-brief-history-of-japanese-sword-and-cutlery-knife-forging/

[7] http://www.japaneseknifedirect.com/aboutseki.html

[8] https://www.japan-guide.com/e/e2127.html

[9] http://www.history.com/topics/samurai-and-bushido

[10] https://en.wikipedia.org/wiki/Respect_for_the_Aged_Day

[11] https://www.lonelyplanet.com/japan/kyoto/attractions/kiyomizu-dera/a/poi-sig/402676/356698

[12] https://www.japan-guide.com/e/e3901.html

[13] https://kyoto.travel/en/shrine_temple/131

[14] https://en.wikipedia.org/wiki/Hello_Kitty

[15] http://news.bbc.co.uk/2/hi/asia-pacific/6932801.stm

[16] https://www.japan-guide.com/e/e3921.html

[17] https://www.japan-guide.com/e/e3902.html

[18] https://iamaileen.com/understand-japanese-geisha-geiko-maiko-define/

[19] https://en.wikipedia.org/wiki/Geisha#Stages_of_training

[20] https://iamaileen.com/understand-japanese-geisha-geiko-maiko-define/

11

Day 11: Bamboo Grove, Golden Pavilion, Nishiki Market, Hip Café, and Wagyu Dinner

Our day began with breakfast at the hostel (which was included in the price). There was a wide variety of warm, cold, Japanese, and foreign dishes. There were many guests in the kitchen at any given time, and even though each guest washed their own dishes, everything was very organized and clean.

During breakfast, we discussed our plans for the day. Our friends wanted to go to a place that offers a geisha makeover. There are a few places in Kyoto that offer a full geisha or maiko makeover experience. The makeover includes wearing the traditional clothes, makeup, and hairstyle.

The traditional maiko dress is a colorful kimono with a bright *obi* (a traditional fabric belt tied in a traditional knot) and wooden sandals[1]. The geisha is dressed in a more subtle colored kimono and raised wooden sandals. The maiko's makeup is a white base, red lipstick, and red and black colors for the eyes and eyebrows. Although it's common to associate this makeup with a geisha, usually a geisha only wears this makeup during special occasions. Depending on the makeover place, the total process can take up to a few hours.

My husband and I had different plans for the day. We wanted to explore Kyoto some more. First, we went to a bus stop to catch bus number 11. The bus stop had a screen that showed when the bus was 5, 3, and 1 minutes away. That is so convenient, I wish every bus stop had that feature.

The bus ride took approximately 45 minutes until we arrived at our destination: the Arashiyama bamboo grove. Arashiyama is a known tourist spot that attracted many people in the past millennium due to its beautiful natural area. The river provides a lovely setting as well as an opportunity to get a pleasure boat ride. A short walk from the river there are many restaurants and cafés, and finally, the bamboo grove[2].

When we got off the bus, it was raining, but thankfully it wasn't windy. Right next to the bus stop we found a shop that sells an ice cream we longed to try: black sesame ice cream. The ice cream has a dark grey color and a flavor similar to tahini or halva. Even though it was raining, we enjoyed the ice cream very much. We also liked the sign in the shop displaying how you can hold a tofu ice cream (or tofu soft cream) upside down.

Top Left: a screen at a bus stop. Bottom Left: Arashiyama. Top Right: black sesame ice cream. Bottom right: display at an ice cream shop.

It was still raining when we entered the bamboo grove, but I felt like the rain only enhanced the colors of the beautiful surroundings. The sea of umbrellas on the path gave a gorgeous contrast to the green columns. The bamboo grove is so different from any other forest I've ever been to. The bamboos weren't very dense, but each one had such a vibrant green color. The path had a brown fence on both sides that provided glimpses of the trees while we were walking.

143

Arashiyama bamboo grove.

For Japanese, bamboos aren't only pretty to look at, but they are also a part of their culture and landscape. Bamboo grows throughout Japan due to the warm and humid climate, so they are commonly used in construction and in many Japanese dishes. Bamboos are very strong, and they symbolize prosperity, purity, and innocence[3]. Owing to the strong roots of the bamboo, it was once believed that a bamboo grove is the safest place to be during an earthquake.

Interestingly, out of all the plants in the world, bamboo has the fastest growth rate. Under certain conditions it can grow up to 91 cm in 24 hours[4]. Although bamboos reach their maturity in 3–5 years, they can survive 120 years in the wild.

When we reached the end of the bamboo grove trail, we noticed there were some construction signs on the street to the left. It was a little crowded in the grove, so we went to see what was under construction. When we arrived, we saw an entrance to a park (Arashiyama Park) and no one around. It seems that the park wasn't a part of the construction. We were so lucky to have the park to ourselves. It was a lovely way to continue our stroll. All the flowers in the park were covered with raindrops and the trees provided some shelter from the rain.

Arashiyama Park.

After checking the shops in the area, we headed towards the bus stop to catch a bus towards our next destination: *Kinkakuji* Zen Temple, the golden pavilion (open every day between 9AM to 5PM), which is located not too far from the bamboo grove. The temple used to be part of the shogun Yoshimitsu's retirement complex[5]. The pavilion was set on fire and destroyed in 1950 and rebuilt in 1955. The structure that can be seen today is a three-story building with the top two floors completely covered with gold leaf.

Each one of the pavilion floors is built using a different architectural style. The first is in the style used for palaces during the Heian period. The first floor holds a statue of Shaka Buddha that can be seen from the outside through the window. The second floor is built in the style of samurai residences. The third floor is built in the style of traditional Chinese Zen.

We got off the bus and walked towards the cashier to pay the ¥400 admission fee (per person). The walk towards the cashier was already beautiful since the trees and ground were covered with bright green moss. Moss needs a humid climate to thrive, so Japan makes an ideal environment for moss to develop and grow[6]. Similar to bamboo, moss is also a part of the Japanese culture. Not only because moss provides an esthetic sight when it covers the country with vibrant green, but also because it is revered for its age. Moss doesn't grow fast, and any object that is covered by moss takes a long time to develop. Moreover, moss is tied with the art of Zen. Having a Zen garden without any moss is unlikely.

Left: Kinkakuji Zen Temple. Right: a moss covered tree.

We were delighted that we got a chance to see these moss-covered trees because one of the destinations we didn't have time to visit during this trip is a moss garden (Saiho-Ji temple). This garden is considered as the highlight of the Saiho-Ji temple with approximately 120 different moss species[7].

Good to know: Saiho-Ji temple (moss garden) requires a reservation. The reservation process is a bit complicated. I suggest following the instructions on digjapan.travel

Even though the moss-covered trees were very attractive, it wasn't the highlight of our trip to the golden pavilion. As soon as we saw the beautiful golden pavilion, surrounded by a small pond, large trees, and purple irises, we realized why it is such a popular tourist site. It is absolutely stunning. The greenery looked like a frame that captures the beauty of the golden pavilion. The amazing thing, in my opinion, is the Japanese ability to design gardens. Each angle revealed a glorious new sight. While walking through the gardens, the amount of thought and work that went into the design and maintenance of the gardens was very apparent.

Good to know: Although taking photos of Kinkakuji, the golden Zen temple is allowed, there are areas with signs that prohibit the use of tripods.

We continued through the garden trail that led us to the Sekkatei teahouse. The Sekkatei teahouse was built in the Kinkakuji gardens during the Edo period. It was still a little chilly outside, and a tea break was a wonderful idea. Similar to the teahouse we visited in Tokyo, the Sekkatei teahouse also offers matcha tea and a small dessert for ¥500. The teahouse is a wooden structure with a red interior. It has large sliding doors that were kept open. The doors pointed at the gardens, so guests could enjoy their break while observing the gardens.

The dessert they served, although not as tasty as the dessert in Tokyo, was so pretty. It was a sugary white square with the shape of the temple and mountains on its top side, and two edible gold squares. The matcha was as good as it can be. Overall, I enjoyed this teahouse more than the one in Tokyo, since the atmosphere was much better. Also, there weren't many people there.

Left: Sekkatei teahouse overlooking the Kinkakuji gardens. Right: a dessert with the shape of Kinkakuji temple.

We left the temple and went to the bus stop. While we were waiting, we started to feel hungry and a little cold. We noticed there was an ice cream shop right next to the station. Except for ice cream, the store also sold fried chicken, croquettes, meats on a stick, hot drinks, and *Takoyaki* soup. Takoyaki is a ball-shaped pancake filled with octopus (tako)[8]. We bought the Takoyaki soup for ¥400. It was very good. It was warm, tasty, comforting, and exactly what we needed.

We hopped on the 12 bus towards Kyoto's kitchen, Nishiki market. Nishiki market consists of more than a hundred shops and restaurants in a long and narrow roof-covered market[9]. The stores in the market sell a variety of items, including exceptionally fresh seafood, pickles, sweets, street food, cookware, and knives.

Good to know: Whatever you choose to explore, most of the items sold in Nishiki market are locally produced.

We entered the market and found our first stop after walking only two meters. We stopped at a food stand that sells *surimi fish cakes*. Surimi fish cakes are made of ground fish. By adjusting their shape and texture, they are used to mimic the taste of lobster, crab, or other shellfish[10]. Besides minced fish meat, surimi may include ingredients such as starch, egg white, oil, seasoning, soy, and MSG. In fact, many people eat some kind of a surimi fish cake without knowing what it is. One such example is crab sticks.

The surimi we bought was steamed surimi (or *Kamaboko*). We took one octopus kamaboko on a stick for the both of us. It was warm and incredibly soft and moist due to the steam. The delicate taste and texture opened up our appetites.

As we finished our fish cake, we stumbled upon our next food stop: tempura and deep-fried panko skewers. We bought an eel, fish tempura, and white fish skewers for ¥1,500. The skewers are served on a plastic plate, and the tempura skewer is topped with a special sauce. After we finished enjoying the skewers, we returned the empty plate for disposal. It is very convenient that food vendors dispose of the trash for you, since there are no public bins nearby.

Left: seafood. Top Right: deep-fried panko skewers. Bottom right: surimi fish cakes sold at Nishiki market.

After filling a small portion of our ever-empty stomachs, we took our time exploring the market. We noticed many vendors sell all imaginable kinds of fish, seafood, and oysters. Some of the vendors had a sign next to the oysters reading "eat now," and so we did. We chose two different oysters for the both of us for a total of ¥1,450. Note, this isn't an insane price for only two oysters. The oysters were huge! We were gestured towards a table behind the fish counter, where we could (quickly) enjoy our oysters with a freshly squeezed lemon juice. We enjoyed the oysters profusely, even though my husband usually doesn't like oysters.

It's not surprising to find such an excellent fish market in Japan. Each year, Japan consumes approximately 10% of all the fish caught in the world, making it the largest fish consuming country in the world per capita[11].

After reaching the end of the market, we turned back and returned to the vendor who sold us the oysters. We noticed he also sells fresh sea urchin in their shell for ¥450 each. We got one for me, since my husband was already full. It was the freshest one I ate in Japan. It was so delicate and delicious. I highly recommend eating it, especially in a fish market!

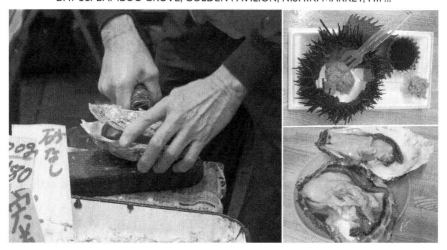

Left: fresh oyster. Top Right: sea urchin. Bottom Right: two fresh oysters on a regular-sized plate.

We went back through the entire market, and also bought lemonade for ¥100, and a jumbo shrimp skewer (3 pcs) for ¥500. I also bought a flower hair pin. During the past days, I noticed wearing flowers in your hair is very popular in Japan. Not only is it popular, but it's also very charming. The store we found has a large variety of different flowery products, and their plastic flowers seem very realistic.

Our last stop before we left the market was Nishiki-koji gallery and café. Here we bought traditional *Kyo-yaki* matcha bowls. Kyo-yaki is the name of pottery made in Kyoto. Kyo-yaki originated in the 16th century when tea ceremonies demanded the production of different pottery styles. During the 17th century, Kyo-yaki evolved, and new distinctive designs were developed. The potters didn't have a high-quality clay for porcelain production, so instead they worked on developing novel shapes and styles. They developed new tools and emphasized the uniqueness of each product. Nowadays, Kyo-yaki provides the best of two worlds: the traditional Japanese design and beauty, along with useful kitchen items. All of the Kyo-yaki principles live to this day and are apparent in the bowls we bought.

The bowls we purchased are produced by Touan (established nearly a century ago). The bowls have a very unique style called *Hanakessho*. Hanakessho literally means flower crystals. The flower crystals are made by using a unique glaze that crystallizes while it cools. There are no two identical flower crystals, which means that each item is unique.

Our next destination was a coffee house called *Elephant Factory Coffee*[12]. Elephant Factory Coffee was featured in a food video we watched on YouTube[13]. It was a bit difficult to find this place, mainly because the sign was almost hidden behind the corner of a building. Going up a set of extremely narrow steps, we reached the second floor of the building where the café is located. The café has a very limited number of seats, and we were lucky to get the last 2 empty seats. We looked around and realized everyone in the café was young and taking pictures of the place, the coffee, and the cheesecakes they serve. We also noticed the café is exceedingly quiet. I am not sure why it is like this, but my husband was ecstatic over this fact.

The coffee in this café is made with beans that are delivered there twice a week after they are roasted by a roastmaster. The coffee is prepared by hand drip and is relatively expensive (¥650-¥750), but it is expensive for a reason. My husband and I both appreciate good coffee and have had good coffee in the past, but we agreed that this was the best coffee we've ever had. Moreover, I think the place is so quiet because people are enjoying their coffee so much that they are left speechless. The mini cheesecake they offered is also something worth noting. It costs only ¥400 but leaves a big impression.

Left: coffee and cheese cake at Elephant Factory Coffee. Right: bowls by Touan.

We went back to the hostel to meet our friends and discuss our dinner plans. Our friend came up with a brilliant idea. He suggested to buy wagyu beef from a nearby butcher and cook it in the hostel's kitchen. We loved this idea! This way we can enjoy a big piece of beef without taking a loan from the bank. My husband and I went to a 7-Eleven store to buy some sides for the meal. We bought a seaweed salad, marinated garlic, and kimchi. We met up with our friends and went to the butcher (located a walking distance to the hostel). There, we bought three different kinds of wagyu beef. They also gave us a piece of fat, so we can use it instead of oil.

We went back to the hostel with all the goodies we got. Luckily, there was only one person in the kitchen, so we had the stove to ourselves. Our friend started frying the meat, while the three of us stood around him and took pictures. The aroma coming from the wagyu beef was so appetizing. We could hardly wait! So, we didn't. As soon as he finished cooking one of the three different wagyu cuts, we sat down and ate it. First, we started with the thinnest pieces. These pieces had the least amount of fat inside. They were so good! They built up my expectation for the rest of the meal. The next cut had the medium amount of fat, and the third had the most fat. My husband loved the thinnest cut the most, while I loved the medium one. We both agreed the third cut was too fatty. Just goes to show you that more doesn't necessarily mean better. Either way, the meal was absolutely fantastic. We were happy and full after a relatively low spending budget of approximately ¥7,000 per couple.

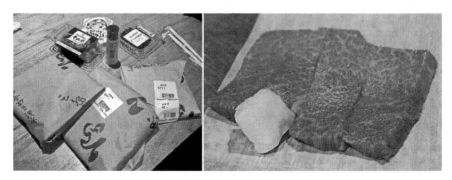

Left: neat packages of wagyu beef. Right: wagyu beef with a piece of fat.

Tip: Buying wagyu beef from a butcher is way cheaper than eating it in a restaurant. Try finding an accommodation with a kitchen to enjoy a nice piece of wagyu beef on a budget. Better yet, I recommend Piece hostel. Even though the room is tiny, the location, staff, breakfast, and kitchen more than make up for it.

Sources:

[1] https://en.wikipedia.org/wiki/Geisha#Appearance

[2] https://www.japan-guide.com/e/e3912.html

[3]   https://www.thoughtco.com/bamboo-in-japanese-culture-2028043

[4] http://www.softschools.com/facts/plants/bamboo_facts/563/

[5] https://www.japan-guide.com/e/e3908.html

[6]   http://theconversation.com/whats-behind-japans-moss-obsession-50500

[7] https://digjapan.travel/en/blog/id=11016

[8] https://en.wikipedia.org/wiki/Takoyaki

[9] https://www.japan-guide.com/e/e3931.html

[10] https://en.wikipedia.org/wiki/Surimi

[11] http://factsanddetails.com/japan/cat24/sub159/item937.html

[12]https://www.tripadvisor.ca/Restaurant_Review-g298564-d6614758-Reviews-Elephant_Factory_Coffee-Kyoto_Kyoto_Prefecture_Kinki.html

[13] https://www.youtube.com/watch?v=PJwqLnPJMLc&t=30s

12

Day 12: Nishiki Market, Love Hotel, and Dotonbori Food Street

After breakfast, we went to the lobby to check out. As usual, my husband and I planned to send our luggage to the next hotel. Our next hotel is located right in the center of Osaka, a 6-min walk from the main food street of Osaka. I was very excited about this hotel because even though it had a wonderful location, the price was reasonable. Also, when I booked it online, it said it's an adult only hotel, so I knew it would be quiet there.

We went to the receptionist and told her we wanted to send our luggage to the hotel we booked in Osaka. While she was filling out the form, she suddenly started to blush. She looked like she wanted to say something, but she avoided eye contact. She called another receptionist for help. After they were done talking, the second receptionist asked us if we know about this hotel. We said we don't know it, but we booked it online in advance. He then explained: "In Japan, there are two kinds of hotels. The first, is a regular hotel. The second is called a 'love hotel'." "Love hotel?" we asked stunned. He looked very uncomfortable, and said: "yes, a hotel you can stay by the hour." He then said he wasn't sure the hotel we booked is a love hotel, but he is suspecting it is. He asked us if we want to send our luggage anyway. We said yes because we already paid for the hotel, and we don't have anywhere else to go.

After this strange beginning to the day, we took our friends to Nishiki market. We wanted them to experience what a fantastic market it is, and we didn't mind going for round two. The only problem was, no one was hungry. While our friends explored the market, we went to have coffee in one of the cafés there. My husband also found a shop that sells black sesame ice cream, so he bought one. I didn't like it, but he said he loved it better than all the previous ones.

We saw several new things that we didn't notice the day before. First, was a sparrow skewer. I didn't even know you can eat sparrows. Turns out you can eat the entire sparrow, except for the feathers. This includes the beak, skull, and even brain[1]. We, however, weren't brave enough to even try.

The second thing we saw was small octopus skewers. The head is said to be filled with an egg. I regret not trying it, but I wasn't hungry. Lastly, we saw a vendor that sells *katsuobushi*. Katsuobushi is dried bonito, used as a seasoning of many Japanese dishes, and a key ingredient in most miso soup broths[2].

Left: black sesame ice cream. Top Right: sparrow skewers. Bottom Right: Katsuobushi at Nishiki market.

The first version of the Katsuobushi was prepared by smoke-drying Skipjack tuna in 1674. The legend tells that during a storm, the ship of a fisherman named Jintaro was wrecked. After the shipwreck, Jintaro has washed up ashore. There, he tried smoking a Skipjack tuna he caught. When he finished, he realized the smoking dramatically improved the fish's taste. A century later, a change in the preparation process of the Katsuobushi was developed. It is said that either a merchant or a Katsuobushi dealer found out his Katsuobushi grown mold. After tasting it, he found out the taste was enhanced. Since then, growing mold on the Katsuobushi is being done intentionally. The growth of the mold causes the Katsuobushi to ferment, similarly to miso and soy sauce. The mold also dries the fish, converts the fat into soluble fatty acids, breaks proteins into amino acids, and protects the fish from other microorganisms.

Our friends stayed in the market to explore some more, while we went back to the hostel. On the basement floor of the hostel there is a café called Drip&Drop. When we checked in to the hostel a few days before, we received a voucher for a free coffee at the Drip&Drop café. We used this voucher and got two hand drip coffees. Although they were not as good as the coffee we drank the day before at the Elephant Factory Coffee, it was still very good. Even more so because it was free. The best thing about the café was the atmosphere. It had a homey feel to it that helped us unwind and relax.

Drip&Drop café.

We joined our friends and took the train to Osaka. The way to Osaka wasn't as picturesque as the other drives we already experienced in Japan, but it was unexpectedly quick. It took us less than 1.5 hours to get to the hotel we booked. However, the unexpected part has just begun.

We got to the hotel and I didn't see the entrance. When we came close to what seemed like a wallpaper covered wall, it suddenly opened. Turned out the wall was actually an automatic sliding door. We entered the reception area, and instead of a front desk, inviting sitting area, and a lobby decor, we saw an empty room with the receptionist sitting behind a wall with a small opening for passing papers. At this point I was starting to get very worried. I realized we booked two nights at a hotel meant for a few hours stay...

Good to know: When booking hotels in Japan, an adults-only hotel can actually mean a love hotel. Read the fine print in order to get more information about the hotel.

Love hotels offer short-time stay and privacy for sexual activities. To optimize the privacy, the interaction with the staff is minimized, and the entrance is usually discrete. The name "love hotel" originates from "hotel love," the first love hotel that was opened in Osaka in 1968[3]. However, the history of the love hotel dates back much further. During the Edo period, teahouses and inns started to add a discrete entrance and tea rooms for prostitutes and clients. It was only a few centuries later, in the 1970s, when the love hotel industry started to peak[4]. Nowadays, the love hotel industry is one of the most profitable in Japan with more than $30 billion a year.

We went to the receptionist and asked her if we came to the correct place. She assured us we did and asked for our passports. While she was taking care of the check-in process, my husband told her that we sent our luggage to the hotel. He asked when we should expect it to arrive. The receptionist sounded stunned, but she couldn't convey her response in English. She called someone she knows who speaks English and gave the phone to my husband. The man told my husband we can't send our luggage to the hotel. My husband said we already have, so how can we get it. In reply, he said we should contact the delivery company and find a place nearby we can send the luggage to.

A little rattled, we continued the check-in process, waiting for our keys.

Little did we know that the hotel doesn't give you a room key. Instead, the receptionist gives you the room number and the door locks when you enter the room. If you wish to leave the room, you need to call the receptionist. The receptionist looks in the security footage to make sure the hall is empty. When the hall is empty, the receptionist unlocks your door and you may leave discreetly.

We decided to give the room a chance. After all, we already paid for it, and the booking is non-refundable. We entered our room, and we noticed it was one of the biggest rooms we saw during our trip. There was a big bed with a large TV screen on the wall in front of it. Behind the bed there was a window. I opened it to let in some fresh air since the room had a funny smell. I looked out the window, and I saw the view was obscured by a high brick wall. Apparently, the confidentiality in this kind of hotel is key, and the brick wall is there to make sure no one can see you (or what you are doing) from the outside.

We continued exploring the room. We went to the washroom and saw there are actually two rooms there. The first had a toilet and a sink. Next to the sink there was any imaginable cream and beauty supply a person may need. The second room was a shower room, and it was huge! The entire room was meant for showering, and there was also a bathtub. Plenty of room to get clean (or dirty).

We went back to the main room and sat on the bed (which had condoms ready for use next to it). We were a little tired, so we turned the TV on. We should have expected it, but the TV mostly had pornography channels. We turned the TV off and called our friends. We agreed to go to some café or restaurant to talk and decide what to do. We called reception and were cleared to leave the room.

We went to a restaurant near the hotel. All of us were shocked by the hotel's concept. While we searched online for a different hotel nearby, my husband and I ordered a curry to share. I'm not sure if the curry was good or not. I felt so bad that I couldn't taste anything. When we finished eating, my husband found another hotel close-by, and we booked it for two nights. We returned to the love hotel to check-out. We were told we are not going to get our money back (and it was true). We later tried getting our money back from the website we booked our stay, but we were denied. Nevertheless, we decided to leave the love hotel.

We went to check-in to Teikoku hotel (¥8,250 per room per night). While we were checking in, we told the receptionist that we sent our luggage from Kyoto to Osaka, but we gave an address they can't deliver to. We asked the receptionist to help us receive our luggage. The receptionist said she will help us. Finally, knowing we arrived at a much more familiar surrounding, we felt relaxed and ready to explore the city. Our first destination was *Dotonbori*.

Dotonbori is Osaka's downtown area located next to Dotonbori-gawa Canal[5]. Dotonbori area is a great representation of what Osaka is about: food and having a good time. Dotonbori is laced with multiple restaurants and bars, and decorated with gigantic advertisement and neon signs that reflect from the canal. Out of all the signs decorating Dotonbori, the most famous one is that of Ezaki Glico company, featuring a running man[6]. This 10 by 20-meter advertisement of a running man with his arms raised in victory was hung there in 2014 to advertise Gilco candy. However, the running man we saw is the 6th version of the Gilco candy advertisement. The first version of Gilco candy advertisement dates back to 1935. Over the years, the running man became a favorite meeting spot, and some even claim the focal point of the area.

Dotonbori, or "Doton canal," was built in 1615. In 1612, a merchant named Doton planned to make a canal to link the Umezu river to a local canal. However, he was killed in 1615 during the Siege of Osaka before completing his plan. Following his death, his cousin completed the canal. The completed canal brought new trade to the area, along with a theater, new restaurants, and teahouses.

Left: Dotonbori canal. Right: Gilco candy advertisement.

This is precisely what attracted us to Dotonbori: the food! Osaka is the best place to eat yourself into bankruptcy. So much so that the Japanese have a word for it, "kuidaore." Kuidaore is a word best associated with Osaka, Japan's kitchen, and we soon realized why.

Our first food destination for the evening was Ganko restaurant. My husband and I ordered assorted crab sushi and 3 tuna nigiri pairs. All for ¥3,280 in total. It was good, but we were starving for more.

As we were walking in the street, we came across several stands that sell Takoyaki. Most of the stands had a very long line. This is not surprising since Takoyaki was initially invented in Osaka[7]. In 1935, a street vendor developed the octopus filled batter shaped into balls, known as Takoyaki. Since then, Takoyaki spread all over Japan with many different topping and recipe varieties. Today, it is one of the favorite comfort foods in Japan, and some claim Osaka makes the best

Takoyaki in Japan.

We got 6 Takoyaki balls in a box and three toothpicks to eat the balls with. The Takoyaki balls were topped with a sweet Teriyaki sauce, mayonnaise, and bonito flakes. They were steaming hot and incredibly soft. A wonderful upgrade for pancake lovers.

Left: assorted crab sushi at Ganko restaurant. Right: Takoyaki at Dotonbori.

Next stop was a different branch of the same restaurant we visited on our second day: Isomaru Suisan restaurant. There, we ordered the same things as last time. We ordered crab miso, salmon sashimi with salmon roe on top, kimchi seafood, and in addition, we ordered tuna sashimi (for a total of ¥2,700 per couple). The food at this restaurant is so good! The miso crab was entirely different than the one in Tokyo, but I can't decide which one was better. In my opinion, the only downside to Isomaru Suisan restaurant is that there is a very strong smoke smell all around the restaurant (coming from the grilling stations).

Left: tuna sashimi. Right: crab miso at Isomaru Suisan restaurant.

Last stop for the day was Honolulu Coffee. Honolulu Coffee is located on the second floor overlooking the canal. My husband and I ordered 2 coffees and cheesecake to share. We sat next to the window to enjoy the view. It was already dark outside, and Dotonbori was filled with dancing neon lights reflecting off of the canal. Many boats crossed the canal while we sat there. If only the coffee and cake were any good, it would have been a perfect place.

When we came back to the hotel the receptionist told us she had taken care of our luggage, and that the delivery address had been changed to this hotel. That was so great! We didn't have to stress over this issue anymore and could enjoy our vacation without any reservations.

Sources:

[1] http://dr-hato.blogspot.ca/2011/10/weird-or-disgusting-food-series-sparrow.html

[2] http://www.tokyofoundation.org/en/topics/japanese-traditional-foods/vol.-15-dried-bonito

[3] https://en.wikipedia.org/wiki/Love_hotel

[4] https://en.wikipedia.org/wiki/Love_hotel

[5] https://www.jnto.go.jp/eng/regional/osaka/dotonbori.html

[6] https://www.osakastation.com/dotonbori-area-the-bright-heart-of-osaka/

[7] https://livejapan.com/en/article-a0001178/

13

Day 13: Osaka Castle, Karahori Shopping Street, Tea Ceremony, and Rooftop Garden

The history of Osaka can be traced back at least 1,400 years[1]. Due to Osaka's location on the Seto Inland Sea, and next to where two rivers converge, it became a trade center that gathers merchants from all over Asia. The merchants introduced Osaka with new crafts and technologies that quickly spread all over Japan. Along with the new technologies, Japan was also introduced to Buddhism. In 593, the first Buddhist temple, Shitenno-Ji Temple, was built in Osaka. During the Heian period (794–1185), many Buddhist temples were constructed in Osaka and Kyoto. Today Buddhism is one of the most predominant religions in Japan.

During the 14th century, following the rise of the Minamoto clan, Osaka and its surroundings were ravaged by war. A century later, in 1496, the Ishiyama Hongan-Ji temple was built. This temple was built as a fortress by *Ikkō-ikki*, a league of warrior monks who opposed the samurai rule[2]. In 1576, the temple came under siege by a warrior and government official named Nobunaga. The siege lasted 11 years; the longest siege in Japan's history. The siege ended with a surrender followed by the burning of the temple. In 1583, Nobunaga's successor, Hideyoshi, began the construction of Osaka castle on the ruins of the

Hongan-Ji temple. The structure was completed almost 15 years later, and it is said that the outer walls were built with more than 500,000 stones. However, the castle was burnt to the ground during the Winter siege and Summer war less than 20 years after it was built.

Osaka castle is where we decided to start our day. When we arrived there, it was still morning, and there weren't many tourists there. The castle is located on a hill and requires some climb. Probably this is the reason this location was so strategic and desirable. The castle seen today dates back to 1931 when it was reconstructed with funds raised by the citizens of Osaka. The castle was modeled by a painting from the late 16th century.

On the grounds of the castle, we bought a Kobe minced meat cutlet stick for ¥350. We also bought black sesame and Sakura mochi ice cream cones. It was a great breakfast, especially on a warm day like this.

While we were enjoying our ice creams, we heard actual screams. We followed the sound of the screams and found an actor dressed as a samurai. He was roaring and yelling, challenging the tourists to take a picture with him. He noticed my husband and started challenging him to come closer, but my husband wasn't up to the challenge. Luckily, a group of tourists was, so we could enjoy looking from the side.

Left: Osaka castle. Center: black sesame and Sakura mochi ice cream cones. Right: an actor dressed as a samurai.

When we were done exploring the castle, we headed towards a market I found online. For each city we visited, I looked for "hidden gems" online. While I couldn't find any worthwhile hidden gems in the previous cities, I believe I hit the jackpot on this one. I am talking about Karahori shopping street (Karahori walker).

Karahori shopping street is stretched over 800 meters. This shopping street is mainly for locals and usually isn't a tourist destination. The shopping street is also home to one of the Super Tamade supermarket stores. Super Tamade is a supermarket with very low prices. During sales, prices can be as low as ¥1[3]. Not only is it cheap, but it's also usually open 24/7 and is decorated by neon and LED lights.

We finished exploring the supermarket before our friends did, so we went outside to wait for them. I strolled down the street, while my husband stood outside of a shisha bar and waited. While I was walking, I heard someone come to my husband and start talking to him. I turned back and realized the friendly guy from the shisha bar came out to talk to us.

He asked us about our trip and where we were from. Then he said that if we have some free time, he can take us to his friend's shop for a private tea ceremony, for free. He said his friend is a tea sommelier. Honestly, it was the first time I heard of a "tea sommelier." I am familiar with a wine sommelier, who works at fine restaurants and pairs wine to food, but what is a tea sommelier? From the context, I realize he meant someone who is very knowledgeable about different teas and knows the exact way to bring out their distinct flavors and aromas.

We were amazed by how friendly this guy is, and we told him we would love to take part in a tea ceremony. I called our friends to join us, and we followed him a few meters down the street on the opposite side from the supermarket. We entered a small tea shop that we overlooked before. Not exactly overlooked, we did enter right before we went to the grocery store; however, without understanding anything about Japanese tea, we didn't stay there long.

When we entered the store, the guy talked with his friend who is an elderly man. The man seemed a bit tired and displeased, but he was very kind to us. He gestured towards a small table at the back of the store, and we followed his welcome and sat down. Then, he called his wife, and somehow without any additional words spoken between them, she turned on the kettle and made the table. When she finished, in front of us were 4 regular sized cups, 4 small cups, a measuring cup, and a teapot.

The "tea sommelier" then followed a long process of pouring liquids from the teapot between different cups back and forth. He followed this process to make sure the water is in the exact temperature it should be. When he finished, he told us we could drink the tea. The tea had an intense and amazing flavor. When I drank it, I realized that until this point I've never drank a proper green tea.

The same leaves were covered in water at different temperatures three more times. At each time, the tea tasted totally different. For me, it felt less like a tea ceremony and more like a magic show. How could the same tea leaves taste so different each time?

When we finished drinking the fourth teacup, the sommelier fished the tea leaves from the teapot and placed them on four plates. He poured some soy sauce on top and put a small fork on each plate. He smiled mischievously, served us the plates, and said "challenge." At this point I was in a big dilemma. I had such a pleasant taste in my mouth, and I didn't want to ruin it by eating bitter leaves. On the other hand, this person was so welcoming and friendly. He gave us a fantastic experience, and for free! I decided I am going to eat the tea leaves, even if I don't like them. I took a forkful of leaves, and quickly put it in my mouth while closing my eyes and preparing for the worst. To my surprise, the worst didn't come.

On the contrary, this was the highlight of this experience! The tea leaves didn't have any bitterness left in them. They had a very delicate flavor that reminded me of seaweed in soy sauce. I was so happy I took on the challenge.

A tea ceremony at Karahori shopping street.

When the ceremony was over, the sweet couple asked us where we were from. We told them, and they took out a notebook that had a list of all the people who visited them for a tea ceremony. We were surprised to discover there were more than 4,700 people above us on the list. Later, we asked about the tea leaves. The sommelier told us they were young tea leaves collected only 10 days ago. I don't think I've ever tasted tea made from such fresh leaves. It was so cool.

We were very grateful for the experience, so we bought several teas from them. They gave us instructions on how to make the tea correctly (the way he did during the ceremony) and told us to keep the leaves in the freezer for up to 6 months.

When we left the store, the guy from the shisha bar came to talk to us again. We thanked him for telling us about this shop and arranging the ceremony. We asked him if there are more cool places like this we can visit. Places that are known to the locals but unknown to tourists. He gave us a list of several spots. He also recommended we go up the street to a small organic store and buy strawberries and *ume* juice (salty plum juice). He said the strawberries are completely different than in other countries.

We said goodbye and headed to the store he recommended. We bought the strawberries and the juice, and we tasted them as soon as we left the store. The strawberries were indeed different than the ones we are familiar with. They had a softer texture and a different flavor. I'm not sure if I liked them more than the ones I know, but they were a tasty snack. Then, my husband and I tried the juice. It was so sour and salty! We couldn't handle more than one gulp. Perhaps we bought a vinegar instead of juice, but we threw it away.

We bought a few more things in the market: a couple of croissants at a store named "Green," but they weren't very fresh. We also bought a small tuna sashimi tray for ¥500 from a fish vendor in the shopping street. Although the tuna was very fresh, it wasn't great. Our friends bought a salmon tray, and they said it was delicious!

From Karahori shopping street we turned right on Tanimachi-suji street and entered an udon noodles restaurant. At the restaurant, my husband and I ordered two different udon noodles for ¥1,000 each. Before we received the noodles, we got two disposable aprons. This is always a great start for me. It means that you can, and are even expected, to pig-out a little. When we got our udon noodles, I understood the need for the aprons. The sauce was so thick and comforting. With each slurp of the noodles, the sauce went everywhere. It was a delicious and fun experience. My husband says it was one of the noodle highlights for him during the trip.

Udon noodles.

Our next destination was Kuromon Ichiba market. This market was first established in 1902 and named after a nearby market[4]. Today Kuromon Ichiba is a covered market that stretches over 580 meters. The market offers a large variety of fruits, vegetables, and seafood, for individuals and restaurants alike.

Sadly, we weren't too hungry after lunch, so we only bought salmon and crab nigiri from one of the shops (for ¥600). Our friends bought salmon sashimi. The nice thing about this fish store is that they sell different fish and seafood and have a large variety of sushi in the back of the store. Next to the large sushi display there are tables you can dine at. This offers a quick and tasty adventure where you can jump from one extremely fresh food experience to the next.

Next, my husband and I headed towards Namba Parks, while our friends headed to a different destination. Namba Parks was also mentioned in the list of "the hidden gems" of Osaka. Built in 2003, Namba Parks is a shopping mall and office compound stretched over 8 above-ground (and 1 basement) floors[5]. Even though the mall offers similar store and restaurants to different places in Japan, it also provides a unique rooftop experience. On each one of the 8 floors there is a rooftop garden that provides green space in the center of the city. Some of the many features of the garden include trees, waterfalls, flower beds, and even ponds.

Namba Parks is only a 10-minute walk from Kuromon Ichiba market, so we decided to walk there. On our way, we accidentally stumbled upon another destination I had on my list of things to see in Osaka. This destination is called Sennichimae Doguyasuji Shopping Street, and it is exactly halfway between Kuromon Ichiba and Namba Parks. Sennichimae Doguyasuji is nicknamed "Kitchenware Street." Even though it stretches over only 150 meters, it has a high number of shops with kitchen accessories, utensils, and Japanese knives for both private and restaurant uses[6].

For us, Sennichimae Doguyasuji was a perfect place for some last-minute souvenir shopping. We also bought some kitchen accessories for ourselves. We were also interested in seeing the knife stores, since before going to Japan we planned to purchase knives in this shopping street after we read it has a great selection and competitive prices.

Tip: Seemingly, Doguyasuji street does have a great selection of knives and reasonable prices, but I still recommend purchasing a knife in a smaller store where you can get a lot of attention and help. We purchased our knives at Hayakawa Hamonoten. Not only did we get the knives for a good price, but we also received a helpful shopping experience and a lesson for life.

When we finished our shopping spree, we stopped at NAKAO Factory Works & Coffee Stands for some coffee. The staff was very friendly and welcoming. We ordered a hand drip made from their original blend. It was an okay hand drip coffee.

After leaving the coffee place, we continued strolling in the shopping street. We noticed one store that sold plastic food items that had a huge plastic chicken leg grilling in a massive plastic fire. The plastic chicken caught our attention, and we entered the store. It was a food replica specialty store that sold fake food magnets, souvenirs, and restaurant display options.

Left: sushi at Kuromon Ichiba market. Right: a huge plastic chicken leg grilling on a plastic fire at Doguyasuji street.

Plastic fake food is actually prevalent in Japan. It isn't only made from plastic, it is also commonly made from wax and resin[7]. The fake food is used in many restaurant street displays. It's a great way to showcase the most popular dishes in the restaurant to attract passersby. The fake food was first developed during the 1920s by artisans and candle makers in Japan in order to eliminate the need for a menu at a restaurant. The fake food can last for years and years. For this reason, the market share of fake food in Japan is on the decline. However, it's still estimated to be very high (estimated to have revenues of billions of Yens per year).

We continued our walk to Namba Parks and were surprised to find out that the entrance to the garden was easily accessible from the street. When we entered the park, we felt like we left the city. The park is well thought out. It has so many different flower beds and various natural elements. It's only when you lift your head or walk to the edge of the garden when you realize you are right in the center of a very urban setting.

Namba Parks.

We climbed up from one story to the next. Although each story wasn't very big, it was totally different than the previous one. We continued our climb all the way to the top, and we reached it right as the sun was starting to set. We were almost completely alone in the garden, and it was very romantic.

Tip: For a romantic destination, try getting to Namba parks before the sunset, since the park offers a nice view of the city, especially during twilight.

The wind was starting to pick up, so finally, we left the garden and entered the mall. There, we went to Costa Mesa (located on the 4th floor) for a dessert. We got the Dutch baby pancake for ¥900, along with two cups of Earl Grey tea. It was a lovely way to end our romantic stroll in the gardens.

Left: the view from Namba Parks during sunset. Right: a Dutch baby pancake at Costa Mesa.

For dinner, we went to Dotonbori again. It seems like the food selection there is endless, and we craved sampling as much of it as we can. We decided to go to a conveyor belt sushi restaurant named Daikisuisan. As I mentioned before, the conveyor belt sushi was invented in Osaka. We were curious to see if a conveyor belt sushi restaurant is better in Osaka then in Tokyo. Soon we found out it isn't. Not that the restaurant wasn't good, but it also left a feeling of promise unfulfilled when we left. In my opinion, conveyor belt sushi is best for people who really want some sushi and are in a hurry. To truly enjoy a sushi experience, it's better to go to a sushi restaurant, or better yet, to a fish market. I don't believe this particular restaurant is very cheap. My husband and I had 20 plates with 1-2 nigiri each for a total of ¥5,300. The good thing I can say about the restaurant is that the menu is very diverse, and the line to enter moves very fast.

Our final stop for the evening was Pasela Resorts. Pasela resorts is an entertainment facility that offers Karaoke, dining, and a private party venue. It is located on the second floor, although it has a display window on the ground floor. The display window features a bread dessert similar to what we ate in Squall café in Tokyo. When we entered the dining area, we noticed we are the only customers there. What a huge contrast to what was going on in all the ground floor restaurants in Dotonbori. We were told they have a Free Drink Bar. For ¥500 you can have as many of their juices, hot beverages, soups, and ice cream. The Drink Bar doesn't offer alcoholic drinks. There is no time limit, and you are free to enjoy a restful break. I don't know how long we sat there, but we sampled much of the Free Drink Bar menu.

The exciting part was going to the washroom. Since Pasela resorts is also a Karaoke place, there are showers on the way to the washroom. The washroom itself was cool too. When I approached the toilet, the lid automatically opened. What a nice welcome! Next to the sink there were a ton of beauty supplies such as hair ties, makeup removers, and more. I wonder how their Karaoke is.

Tip: For a more quiet and relaxing experience in Dotonbori street, the above ground restaurants and cafés offer somewhat of a break from the crowd.

Sources:

[1] https://osaka-info.jp/en/page/osaka-history

[2] https://en.wikipedia.org/wiki/Ishiyama_Hongan-ji

[3] https://trip101.com/article/8-shopping-spots-in-Osaka-to-visit

[4] https://www.osakastation.com/kuromon-ichiba-market/

[5] https://inhabitat.com/japans-namba-parks-has-an-8-level-roof-garden-with-waterfalls/

[6] https://www.osakastation.com/sennichimae-doguyasuji-shotengai/

[7] https://en.wikipedia.org/wiki/Fake_food

14

Day 14: Market, Shopping Street, Coney Island/Paris of Japan, and Last Dining Experiences

For our last day, we decided to have as many of the different foods we liked best during our trip. So, the first thing we did in the morning was going to Kuromon Ichiba market. We arrived only 15 minutes after the market opened, and what a perfect time it was. The market was mostly empty, as all the shops and vendors prepared for the day. We went to one of the shops and bought 10 tuna and salmon nigiri topped with salmon roe for ¥3,000. The fish looked so fresh and inviting. There were generous pieces of fish covering the rice underneath. We sat in the sitting area, eager to try the nigiri. Both the tuna and salmon nigiri were unbelievably delicious. I am not sure which one was better. They were so soft that they almost melted in my mouth. They were extremely fresh! To this day, I am not sure if it was the best sushi we had in Japan, but for sure in the top two.

Tuna and salmon nigiri topped with salmon roe at Kuromon Ichiba market.

Tip: Going to Kuromon Ichiba fish market close to the opening hours (9AM) is highly recommended. The market is mostly empty, and the fish is exceptionally fresh and delicious.

When we finished and went outside, we saw how a big piece of salmon fillet was precisely cut into identical sashimi pieces. I must have spent 5 minutes staring at this process. The small OCD part of me was delighted.

Another cool thing we noticed in the market was a few stalls that sell *Fugu*, or pufferfish. In general, compared to Tokyo and Kyoto, Osaka has more places offering Fugu. We enjoyed looking and thinking about Fugu, but we didn't dare to try it.

Good to know: Fugu (pufferfish) has a very toxic poison in its organs. Therefore, the preparation of Fugu is highly regulated in Japan. Only chefs who trained for at least three years, and were qualified, are allowed to prepare Fugu[1]. Preparing Fugu at home is illegal. A failure to remove some of its poisonous organs or improper handling may result in death. Each year, there are about 20 cases of Fugu poisoning in Japan. Some of these cases result in death[2].

Good to know: The liver of the pufferfish is considered the most flavorsome part, but it holds the greatest risk for poisoning.

Even though Fugu is highly toxic, it is a Japanese dish enjoyed across Japan for hundreds of years[3]. Through the years, Fugu resulted in countless deaths, which led to its ban between 1570s to 1870s. Nowadays, it is not only enjoyed by adrenaline seekers, but it is also enjoyed for its flavor and nutritional properties.

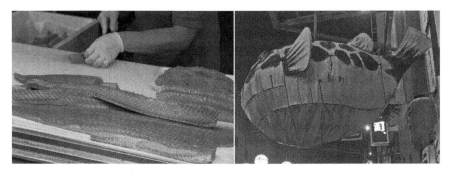

Left: salmon fillets cutting. Right: a Fugu (pufferfish) sign.

Fugu has also entered the Japanese culture in one short story. In the story, three men prepare a Fugu stew. The men wanted to make sure the stew was safe to eat, so they gave some of it to a tramp. The tramp seemed to be fine, so the three men went to eat the stew themselves. A few hours passed, and the three men reencountered the tramp. The tramp was pleased to see that the men are in good health. What the three men didn't know, was that the shrewd tramp hid the stew instead of eating it. After seeing the men were okay, he went back to finally eat the stew.

Before leaving the market for our next destination, we found a vendor who sells breaded fried food on a stick. We bought a crab leg for ¥350. Although the crab leg was cold, it was still very tasty and fresh.

Our next destination was the same shopping street we visited a day before: Doguyasuji. We wanted our friends to experience it as well. Also, when we came back to the hotel in the evening the day before, we realized we left a bag at the coffee shop there. The bag had presents we bought for our families, so it was important for us to retrieve it. My husband went to get the bag, while I waited with our friends outside. It felt so long until he came back. Turns out the workers there didn't understand English (or my husband's mime ability). Thankfully, Google Translate came to his rescue. He wrote down "I left a bag here yesterday." He showed them the translation on his screen, hoping Google didn't write anything offensive. Following, the worker went to the back of the shop and came back with the bag.

We bought a few more things, and while our friends continued their shopping, we stumbled upon a caricature artist at a shop called Osaka Wonder Land. My husband and I thought it would be a fun memento of our trip to Japan, so we asked for a caricature of the two of us. While the caricaturist was drawing, we noticed the edges of the drawing where we could see how he drew our hair. It seemed very good! I was becoming very excited to see the final result. Then, as time passed, I saw his expression was increasingly more mischievous. At this point I was starting to worry. What is he going to do? I have a big nose and small eyes, but still, I want to hang this caricature on the wall. Finally, he was done, and I was anxious to see the result. First thing I noticed was an uncanny portrait of my husband! I feel like he captured his spirit in this caricature. My caricature, on the other hand, was a disappointment. Even though my hair looked gorgeous, it had no resemblance to me. Now it hangs on the wall in our home office and still makes me smile every time I look at it (especially when I look at the caricature of my husband). So, our goal was definitely achieved.

As lunchtime approached, we decided to have Ramen and gyoza for the last time (this trip). We went to Osaka Ohsho restaurant, which has both items on their menu. Turns out, the translation of the restaurant's name is "The King of Gyoza in Osaka[4]." The restaurant proudly defends its title with its lovely Gyoza. It was certainly worth going there for our last Gyoza. Sadly, I can't say the same for the Ramen. For me, it was just average, and wasn't even in the same league as the Ramen we ate in Tokyo's Ramen Street.

Left: Ramen. Right: Gyoza at Osaka Ohsho restaurant.

After we finished our lunch, we looked online for a place nearby that makes siphon coffee. We found a café named Grande Coffee located only 2 minutes away. When we got there, my husband and I ordered two siphon coffees. We didn't wait long before the coffees arrived in charming cups. The cups were decorated with gold and came with a matching tiny milk pitcher. The café offered a lovely relief from the warm day outside. We sat there for a long time just resting and thinking to ourselves. The only downside was that the air was filled with cigarette smoke.

Siphon coffee at Grande Coffee.

After our long break, we took a train towards Shinsekai. Shinsekai is a district in Osaka that was developed during the 1910s following a successful industrial exposition that was held in the area[5]. The exposition brought millions of people to the area in less than six months. Shinsekai, which literally means "new world", was modeled after two other new world cities: Coney Island in New York, and Paris in France. The northern half of Shinsekai, modeled after Paris, contains Tsutenkaku tower. Tsutenkaku tower was modeled after the Eiffel tower, and at the time was the tallest building in Asia[6]. Although the original tower was destroyed during WWII, the tower that can be seen today was reconstructed not long after, in 1956. As the Eiffel tower is the symbol of Paris, the Tsutenkaku is the symbol of Shinsekai.

Good to know: Shinsekai is considered the least safe neighborhood in Japan, with a high prostitution rate[7]. The areas surrounding it have numerous homeless settlements.

When we got there, we were not aware of the reputation this area had, although it did seem strange that the area was mostly deserted. Fortunately, we didn't encounter any safety concern during our visit. The district did not seem dangerous to us. We noticed there were many restaurants there. As in Dotonbori, in a tiny stretch of street

185

a person can sample a broad spectrum of the Japanese cuisine. The Shinsekai area is mostly known for a dish called *Kushikatsu*. Kushikatsu is battered and deep-fried meat, seafood, or vegetable skewers[8].

Good to know: In Osaka, it is common to have a dish named Kushikatsu that comes with a dipping sauce. The sauce is often shared between customers. For this reason, there is an unwritten rule on how to eat the Kushikatsu. The rule dictates "don't dip twice." In other words, you can only dip a skewer you haven't eaten yet.

Even though the Shinsekai area was filled with many restaurants, there was a single restaurant that caught our eyes: Yokozuna Tsutenkaku shop. Yokozuna Tsutenkaku shop is decorated from outside with murals of sumo wrestlers. Not only is the outside of the restaurant inspired by sumo wrestlers, but the menu is also inspired by them. The restaurant's display window was filled with plastic dishes of enormous size. A simple Japanese omelet looked like it could feed a family of four.

Sumo is a type of martial art that was invented in Japan. Sumo dates back at least to the seventh century[9]. To this day, sumo is professionally practiced solely in Japan[10]. During a sumo wrestling match, the goal is to push the opponent outside of a circular ring or into contact with the ground with any part of their bodies other than their feet. There are no weight categories in sumo, so often there is an advantage to great body mass. Professional sumo wrestlers follow strict traditional rules for every aspect of their lives. The rules include the way they train, how they dress, their hairstyle, and even what they eat.

Sumo wrestlers usually don't eat breakfast, and their first meal of the day is during lunch. Their traditional lunch is a giant fish, meat, and vegetable stew named *chankonabe* with a side of rice and beer.

Following lunch, the wrestlers are expected to take a nap. The goal of this regime is to help the wrestlers gain plenty of weight. Similarly, the wrestlers have dinner right before they go to sleep. In total, a sumo wrestler eats 20,000 calories per day, almost 10 times the recommended diet of a grown man[11].

Next to Yokozuna Tsutenkaku, we noticed a few statues of Billiken. Billiken is "The God of Things as They Ought to Be[12]." Even though it's easy to spot Billiken statues in Japan, and even though it has a slight resemblance to Buddha, it is actually not Japanese. Its appearance was invented by an art teacher in the early 1900s, and it is the mascot of Saint Louis high school and university. Later, it was adopted in Japan as the god of things as they are supposed to be.

My husband and I were almost out of JPY by this point in our trip. Turns out, when we calculated how much the trip will cost us, we were off by ¥10,000. We went to a 7-Eleven branch to withdraw money using our VISA credit card. We thought that the exchange rate will be much higher, but we were pleasantly surprised to find out we only paid extra Canadian $5.75 for the withdrawal (on top of the official conversion rate). It was a great relief to have spending money again. Now we were ready to continue exploring.

Tip: If you plan to withdraw money in Japan, check online if your credit/debit card can be used in a 7-Eleven ATM[13], since it is a big chain with many branches throughout Japan.

We were starting to feel hungry, but before going to have a few more last Japanese meals we went to Hozenji Temple. Hozenji Temple is located a few minutes walk from Dotonbori. The temple was built during the 1630s[14]. It brought many visitors to the area, which slowly developed into a food and entertainment district. During WWII, the entire temple was destroyed, except for one statue. This was the statue of Fudo Myo-o, a Buddhist deity who helps people achieve enlightenment by burning away their sins[15]. To accomplish this goal, this god is always depicted with an angry and fierce face. However, this particular statue of Fudo Myo-o in Hozenji Temple doesn't look as intense and angry as the rest of Fudo Myo-o statues, because it is completely covered with moss.

Left: a samurai mural at Yokozuna Tsutenkaku shop. Right: Fudo Myo-O statue in Hozenji Temple.

The story says that 80 years ago one lady made a wish to the statue of Fudo Myo-o, and then splashed water at it. When her wish came true, she told everyone she knew about it. Since then, each person who makes a wish from the god splashes water at the statue. This constant wetness makes an ideal condition for moss to thrive[16].

Our last food attractions in Osaka were again experienced in Dotonbori. As I mentioned before, Dotonbori has PLENTY of food choices and destinations to offer. We went to a vendor that makes Yakitori, and we got two chicken Yakitori as an appetizer. They were fresh and juicy, so they definitely served their purpose. They opened up our appetites and left us with a great memory of Yakitori in Japan.

Next, we took our own advice and looked for a restaurant in one of the top floors of Dotonbori. We soon found the perfect place to have our last proper Japanese dinner. The restaurant is called Mitsuru and is located right above a FamilyMart. Mitsuru restaurant offers a fun dining experience. There is a charcoal fire grill in the middle of the table. You can order different cuts of Wagyu beef and grill them to perfection yourself. My husband and I ordered a few different cuts to share. He cooked them, while I enjoyed the show, but mostly I enjoyed the flavor. The meat was so tender and moist. My husband is a grilling master, and with the right cuts his skills are unstoppable. In my opinion, this was the best Wagyu experience I had during this entire trip.

Left: Yakitori at Dotonbori. Right: wagyu beef at Mitsuru restaurant.

Believe it or not, we still had room for dessert. When we left the restaurant, we saw this cute food truck that sells melon-shaped pastries filled with ice cream for ¥400. They proudly display a sign that says they sell the world's second-best freshly baked Melon-pan Ice cream. We stood in a long line, while trying to decide which ice cream flavor to get. We decided to get a single Melon-pan vanilla ice cream for the both of us. I have to tell you, if this is the world's second-best

Melon-pan, I can't wait to try the best one! The Melon-pan looked huge, but it was so airy and delicate that in a single bite you can take a significant portion of it. The temperature and flavor contrast between the freshly baked pan and the cold ice cream was terrific. I wish every ice cream I eat would be served like this.

Our last destination in Dotonbori, and in Osaka, was Pasela resorts. My husband and our friends ordered their famous dessert, while I enjoyed some beverages. I think even if we would have stayed in Osaka for a week, we would still finish each day in Pasela resorts. This place offers such a great escape from the crowd and the noise outside. As a bonus, it also makes a great dessert.

Left: a dessert at Pasela resorts. Right: a freshly baked Melon-pan Ice cream.

With a very heavy heart, it was time for us to go to our final destination in Japan: the hotel (City Hotel Airport in Prince, ¥8,600 per room per night) close to Osaka airport, from where we departed home the next morning. We took a train to get there. The train was both crowded and moved very slowly. However, the long commute gave me time to reflect on the last two weeks. This trip to Japan provided me with a glimpse into a different world. A world with incredible food, hardworking and honest people, and amazing architecture and landscape. I knew deep in my heart that this trip won't easily be forgotten and that it would take some time for me to return to my usual routine. I can't wait for my next trip to Japan.

Sources:

[1] https://en.wikipedia.org/wiki/Fugu

[2] http://factsanddetails.com/japan/cat19/sub123/item649.html

[3] https://savorjapan.com/contents/more-to-savor/eating-fugu-the-deadly-and-delicious-japanese-pufferfish/

[4] https://www.facebook.com/osakaohsho.singapore/

[5] https://www.japan-guide.com/e/e4012.html

[6] http://theonlyblondeinosaka.blogspot.ca/2012/04/shinsekai-osaka-new-world.html

[7] https://en.wikipedia.org/wiki/Shinsekai

[8] https://www.tsunagujapan.com/the-right-way-to-eat-the-famous-osaka-kushikatsu/

[9] http://web-japan.org/kidsweb/virtual/sumo/sumo03.html

[10] https://en.wikipedia.org/wiki/Sumo

[11] https://www.lingualift.com/blog/what-sumo-eat-wrestlers-diet/

[12] http://jpninfo.com/31185

[13] https://www.sevenbank.co.jp/oos/adv/intlcard02/en/

[14] https://www.osakastation.com/hozenji-temple-hozenji-yokocho/

[15] https://en.wikipedia.org/wiki/Acala

[16] https://www.osakastation.com/hozenji-temple-hozenji-yokocho/

15

Destinations List

Day 1 (Tokyo)
- *Nippori* neighborhood.

Day 2 (Tokyo)
- Shopping next to *Ueno* station.
- *Kameido Tenjin* Shrine.
- *Nakamise* shopping street.
- *Sensoji* temple.
- Edo downtown Traditional Crafts Center.

Day 3 (Tokyo)
- *Ueno-onshi-koen* Park (Ueno Park).
- *Ameya yokocho* (Ameyoko).
- Basement food floor (*depachika*) in *Isetan Kaikan* shopping mall.
- Metropolitan Government Building.
- *Golden Gai* nightlife street.
- *Omoide Yokocho* (Yakitori alley).

Day 4 (Tokyo)
- *Tsukiji Hongwanji* temple.
- *Tsukiji* market.
- *Hamarikyu* gardens.
- *Shibuya* crossing.
- *Cat Cafe MoCHA.*
- *Tokyu food show.*

Day 5 (Tokyo)
- UN University farmers' market.
- *Yoyogi* park.
- *Harajuku, Takeshita Dori* street.
- *Harajuku, Cat Street.*
- *Saito-yu* public bath.

Day 6 (Tokyo)
- *Kabukiza* Theatre.
- *Kappabashi* "kitchen town."
- Taitō neighborhood.

Day 7 (Tokyo-Hirayu)
- *Shinjuku* bus terminal.
- Scenic bus drive to Hirayu.
- *Nakamurakan* Ryokan.
- Foot onsen.
- Private outdoor bath.

Day 8 (Hirayu-Takayama)
- Private outdoor bath.
- *Kappabashi* bridge.
- Bus to Takayama.
- *Hida Kokubunji* Temple.

Day 9 (Takayama-Kyoto)
- Morning market.
- Hida folk village.
- Takayama old town.
- Scenic bus drive to Kyoto.
- *Teramachi* street.

Day 10 (Kyoto)
- *Fushimi Inari-Taisha* shrine.
- *Senbon Torii* trail.
- *Hayakawa Hamonoten* knife shop.
- *Kiyomizudera* temple.
- *Pontocho* alley.

Day 11 (Kyoto)

- *Arashiyama* bamboo grove.
- *Arashiyama* park.
- *Kinkakuji* Zen Temple, the golden pavilion.
- *Nishiki* market.
- *Nishiki-koji* gallery and cafe.

Day 12 (Kyoto-Osaka)

- *Nishiki* market.
- Train to Osaka.
- *Dotonbori* street, Osaka downtown area.

Day 13 (Osaka)

- Osaka castle.
- *Karahori* shopping street (Karahori walker).
- *Kuromon* Ichiba market.
- *Sennichimae Doguyasuji* Shopping Street (Kitchenware Street).
- *Namba* parks.
- *Dotonbori* street.

Day 14 (Osaka)

- *Kuromon* Ichiba market.
- *Sennichimae Doguyasuji* Shopping Street.
- *Shinsekai* district.
- *Hozenji* Temple.
- *Dotonbori* street.

16

Good to Know List

- Japan is a cash country. Credit cards are not accepted everywhere. Moreover, not all ATMs accept foreign credit or debit cards[1].

  - In an Izakaya, a customer is expected to order a food and drink item. It is considered rude not to order both[2].

  - It is common for Japanese restaurants to serve an appetizer (*Tsukidashi*). Usually, the Tsukidashi is not free and you may see it on your bill as a "table charge."

  - It is not customary to leave a tip in a Japanese restaurant[3].

  - It is up to you to decide whether you would use any of the additional functions the Japanese toilet provides. Either way, it is always good to know that means **stop**.

  - Smoking is allowed in most restaurants and bars, and in some hotel rooms in Japan even though it is prohibited to smoke in the street. Smoking in the street is only allowed in designated smoking areas[4]. On the upside, there are currently campaigns for making Japan smoke-free by the Olympic games in 2020.

  - A Suica card can be purchased at any JR (Japan Railways) station. The Suica card can be loaded and recharged (with up to ¥20,000) at any automatic ticket vending machine that displays the Suica logo[5]. The vending machine accepts only JPY (cash only). The card can be refunded at a ticket office, but only in the same region it was purchased. For example, if you purchased the card in Tokyo, it belongs to the

Eastern region and can only be refunded in the East JR stations[6]. The Suica card can be used in subway stations in different JR regions. We got our card in Tokyo and used it in Tokyo, Kyoto, and Osaka.

- In Tokyo subway stations, you are typically expected to walk on the left side, unless there is a sign that tells you otherwise. It is important to try and follow this rule to avoid disturbing or bumping into people. This rule also applies outside the station.

- Warm drinks are either sold at a separate vending machine, or have a sticker that says they are warm.

- When visiting a shrine, behave calmly and respectfully. If you are sick, wounded, or in mourning, you should customarily not visit a shrine.

- Near the shrine, there is a purification fountain. You are supposed to take a ladle, fill it with water and rinse both hands. You are then expected to pour some water into your hand and transfer it to your mouth, rinse, and spit the water next to the fountain. You are not supposed to swallow the water[7].

- From our experience, street food is safe to eat. Generally, people often associate street food with poor hygiene. However, in Japan, this is not true. According to the Japan National Tourism Organization (JNTO), the food and tap water in Japan are safe for consumption, including street food[8]. I am very sensitive to food, but in Japan, I did not have any problems despite eating a lot of street food.

- The most popular times to visit Japan are in the spring, when the Sakura (cherry blossom) blooms, and the fall when Japan is covered in autumn colors. While these two seasons are indeed the most appealing times to visit Japan, the weather isn't at its best. We traveled at the beginning of May and the weather was perfect.

- Many restaurants provide a warm steamed towel called *Oshibori* to clean your hands before the meal (some places hand out cold *Oshibori* during the summer). To comply with Japanese etiquette, you should not use the *Oshibori* to wipe the sweat off your face. When you finish cleaning your hands, fold the towel nicely and leave it on the table until the end of the meal so you can wipe your hands once more, on the opposite side of the towel[9].

- Considering Sensoji temple is the oldest temple in Tokyo, it attracts many tourists, both foreign and Japanese. Therefore, it is very crowded at peak hours (during holidays and weekends)[10].

- When visiting a temple in Japan, it is important to behave calmly and respectfully. If you go inside the temple, you'll need to take off your shoes.

- If you plan to light incense at a temple, put the flame out by waving your hand, not by blowing on it.

- Many items sold in Japan (e.g., in stores) display a price tag that doesn't include a tax. When you purchase an item, the tax will be added to the bill. During our trip, the tax was 8%.

- After purchasing items using a tax-free exemption, you mustn't open the bags as long as you are in Japan, and you must have the bags and receipt with you at the airport before leaving Japan. When at the airport, you should show the receipt at the customs counter. For full details about tax-free shopping in Japan visit: http://tax-freeshop.jnto.go.jp/eng/shopping-guide.php

- Japanese whiskey is so good that in 2014, the Yamazaki Single Malt Sherry Cask 2013 won the world's best whiskey title[11].

- It is usually considered rude to eat on the streets in Japan, whereas it is acceptable to eat while sitting on a public bench. However, finding a public bench may turn out as a challenge since public benches are not too common in Japan.

- Different conveyor belt sushi restaurants have a different method to set the price. Some have the same price for each plate, while others have a different price for different plate colors.

- Ginger is used for cleansing the palate between different types of sushi. It is considered very rude to eat sushi and a piece of ginger with it. The wasabi is used to enhance the flavor of the fish and to kill any parasites the fish may have.

- Nigiri sushi already has wasabi in between the fish and the rice, so there is no need to add it yourself[12].

- There are different kinds of karaoke: a private box, where you have a small room to yourself, or karaoke bars, where people sing in front of everyone present. For more guidance on what to expect, visit: *japan-guid.com.*

- You are not allowed to eat in the *depachika* (food floor of a department store). Usually, there is a designated eating area. Another option is to take your food to go.

- Seeing that most establishments in Golden Gai are very small, they commonly have a table charge (Tsukidashi).

- Opening hours for most bars in Golden Gai are 5:30PM Mon-Sat, and 8PM on Sunday.

- Try going to the Yakitori alley in the evening after 4PM, when most Yakitori spots open.

- Each day, only 120 people are allowed to visit the tuna auction in Tsukiji market on a first come- first serve manner. Visitors usually start waiting in line for the Osakana Fukyu Center (Fish Information Center) at the *Kachidoki* Gate a few hours before 5AM. For more information on how to plan a visit to the tuna auction, visit tokyocheapo.com.

- Many sushi chefs in Japan agree that the rice is the most important part of the sushi[13]. For this reason, my husband always prefers ordering nigiri instead of sashimi. This way, he enjoys the perfect harmony between the rice and the fish.

- Tsukiji market is planned to move to Toyosu to make room for the Tokyo 2020 Olympics[14]. The move is scheduled for Sep-Oct 2018[15].

- You are not allowed to enter a tea house with your outdoor shoes. If there is an outside deck, you will be provided with slippers to only be worn there.

- Bathing in a public bath (sento) is done in the nude.

- Some public baths sell tattoo covers for people with tattoos who want to be admitted.

- The sign for the women's locker room in a public bathhouse is red, while the men's is blue.

- You are expected to keep your towel balanced on your head while you are in the bath (at a public bathhouse). It is extremely rude to let your towel touch the water.

- Kappabashi shopping street usually operates between 9AM-5PM.

- There is a discounted rail pass available for tourists. This rail pass has to be purchased from outside of Japan. You may find the full information here: www.japanrailpass.net. We decided not to purchase the pass, because all the bus tickets we bought ended up being cheaper than the pass.

- Slurping noodles is customary in Japan. However, slurping Udon noodles should be done with extra care, since they tend to spray broth if they are being slurped quickly.

- Wagyu beef sometimes carries the name of the region it was raised in. Hida beef, Kobe beef, Matsusaka beef, Yonezawa beef, Mishima beef, and Omi beef are all types of Wagyu beef[16].

- Hida folk village is open every day between 8:30AM to 5PM.

- Fushimi Inari-Taisha shrine (torii trail in Kyoto) becomes very crowded starting from 10AM each day. The peak hours are 10AM-4PM during Saturday and Sunday.

- Although many shrines and temples have food vendors and stalls on their grounds, it is considered highly disrespectful to eat on the grounds away from the food stalls[17].

- Most of the places that offer you items that will later need disposal also have a garbage bin. Some examples include vending machines, convenience stores, or even food vendors.

- Kiyomizudera temple requires a significant hike up many stairs.

- The water from the falls next to Kiyomizudera temple is said to have therapeutic powers. It's said that if a person drinks water from the three streams of the waterfall, he will have better health, longevity, and success in studies[18].

- Saiho-Ji temple (moss garden) requires a reservation. The reservation process is a bit complicated. I suggest following the instructions on digjapan.travel

- Although taking photos of Kinkakuji, the golden Zen temple is allowed, there are areas with signs that prohibit the use of tripods.

- Whatever you choose to explore, most of the items sold in Nishiki market are locally produced.

- When booking hotels in Japan, an adults-only hotel can actually mean a love hotel. Read the fine print in order to get more information about the hotel.

- Fugu (pufferfish) has a very toxic poison in its organs. Therefore, the preparation of Fugu is highly regulated in Japan. Only chefs who trained for at least three years, and were qualified, are allowed to prepare Fugu[19]. Preparing Fugu at home is illegal. A failure to remove some of its poisonous organs or improper handling may result in death. Each year, there are about 20 cases of Fugu poisoning in Japan. Some of these cases result in death[20].

- The liver of the pufferfish is considered the most flavorsome part, but it holds the greatest risk for poisoning.

- Shinsekai is considered the least safe neighborhood in Japan, with a high prostitution rate[21]. The areas surrounding it have numerous homeless settlements.

- In Osaka, it is common to have a dish named Kushikatsu that comes with a dipping sauce. The sauce is often shared between customers. For this reason, there is an unwritten rule on how to eat the Kushikatsu. The rule dictates "don't dip twice." In other words, you can only dip a skewer you haven't eaten yet.

Sources:

[1] https://boutiquejapan.com/money-in-japan/

[2]https://www.tripadvisor.ca/ShowTopic-g294232-i525-k10557342-Okay_to_eat_without_drinking_at_an_izakaya-Japan.html

[3] https://www.swaindestinations.com/blog/tipping-etiquette-when-traveling-in-japan/

[4] http://kyoto.travel/en/traveller_kit/tools_smoking

[5] http://www.jreast.co.jp/e/pass/suica.html?src=gnavi#category05

[6] https://matcha-jp.com/en/836

[7] http://www.japan-guide.com/e/e2057.html

[8] https://www.jnto.org.au/about-jnto/

[9] http://jpninfo.com/25747

[10] https://www.tripadvisor.ca/ShowUserReviews-g1066461-d320447-r203914460-Senso_ji_Temple-Taito_Tokyo_Tokyo_Prefecture_Kanto.html

[11] https://www.washingtonpost.com/news/morning-mix/wp/2014/11/05/japan-beats-scotland-to-win-worlds-best-whiskey-title/?noredirect=on&utm_term=.6a2d97956154

[12] https://blog.opentable.com/2017/sushi-etiquette-dos-and-donts-from-6-top-sushi-chefs-hackdining/

[13] https://lifehacker.com/the-essential-keys-to-making-perfect-sushi-rice-1793199724

[14] https://www.theguardian.com/world/2017/jun/20/worlds-largest-fish-market-will-finally-move-home-says-tokyo-governor

[15] https://www.japantimes.co.jp/news/2017/10/16/national/tokyos-famed-tsukiji-fish-market-moved-next-september-october/#.Wviv OogvxPY

[16] https://en.wikipedia.org/wiki/Wagyu

[17] https://www.japan-guide.com/forum/quereadisplay.html?0+105464

[18] https://kyoto.travel/en/shrine_temple/131

[19] https://en.wikipedia.org/wiki/Fugu

[20] http://factsanddetails.com/japan/cat19/sub123/item649.html

[21] https://en.wikipedia.org/wiki/Shinsekai

17

Tips List

- We looked for hotels that are located close to major transportation terminals, like subways, and train stations. Staying in these locations helped us save time and walking energy since we did A LOT of walking anyways (13 km per day on average). While some websites[1] recommend booking hotels one month in advance, others[2] recommend booking as soon as possible for peak seasons and national holidays.

 - I highly recommend purchasing a data only SIM card[3] to be connected to the Internet and not rely only on Wi-Fi networks. The main advantage for us was the ability to use our phone for navigation: to know what subway line to take, and how to get to our destination. It saved us a lot of time. We purchased a SIM card later in our trip, but you can purchase it at the airport.

 - If you have navigation problems (like me), you can look at a station's floor plan online[4], provided by JR (Japan Railway Company). The floor plan can assist you in finding the correct exit.

 - It is a good idea to stay in a hotel close to transportation station and to avoid a touristy neighborhood. We chose the Nippori neighborhood because it is mostly a residential neighborhood. Staying at a residential area allowed us to explore restaurants visited mainly by locals. These restaurants usually provide more authentic food than restaurants for tourists. Moreover, our hotel was located near Nippori station, which is a central station connected to several subway lines including the JR line.

- If you plan to use buses, subways, or JR trains, it is recommended to get a *Suica* card. It is a prepaid card that saves you the bother of purchasing tickets. Simply use a machine to charge money to your card. Go to the gate, tap the card on the machine and the fair will be automatically deducted from the card. Moreover, it allows you to pay for shopping in the station. This way, you can save time and eliminate the use of change.

- If you want to avoid the golden week, check online to find the exact dates. If you decide to travel during the golden week, plan your stay and book ahead.

- Prepare for crowded situations in advance. Create a system in case someone gets lost, such as going back to a known locatio.

- Dip a nigiri in soy sauce fish side-down so the rice won't fall apart.

- If you are looking for cheap eats, the food floor of the department store *Isetan Kaikan* isn't the best place for you as it is more on the pricey side. Instead, try going to the more affordable *Tokyu*, located in Shibuya.

- Try timing your arrival so you would enter the Metropolitan government building right before the sunset begins. This way, you can enjoy the view of Tokyo and enjoy the romantic atmosphere when the night covers the city.

- The polite way to eat Ramen is while slurping the noodles because this way you convey how delicious it is, while also cooling the noodles[5]. Moreover, the flavors of the Ramen are enhanced when slurping[6]. So, when in Japan, act like a Japanese and slurp away.

- If you want to avoid standing in line for one of the restaurants in Ramen Street, try to arrive after lunch hours (lunch is between 11:30AM-2:00PM) and before dinner hours (starting at 6PM). When we finished eating it was 4PM, on a Saturday during the Golden Week. By that time, the only restaurant with a line was Rokurinsha.

- Right next to Shibuya intersection there is a Starbucks branch located on the second floor. This Starbucks provides a very pretty elevated view of Shibuya Crossing, but it is VERY busy as well[7].

- The UNU market is a nice stop if you are already nearby, or if you live in Tokyo and want some fresh and local products. I wouldn't recommend going out of your way to get there. It is a humble market, with nothing too special.

- If you wish to see the teenage fashion figures in Harajuku, the best time to go is on Sundays. However, be aware that it is also the busiest time to be there.

- If you plan to go to a public bath, it is essential to follow the *bathing etiquette*[8] since manners and respect are very important in Japan.

- Before entering a public bath, it is important to make sure your hair doesn't touch the water, so make sure you bring a hair tie with you.

- Don't tell Japanese people how to do their jobs. Otherwise, they will be highly offended.

- The discounted tickets for a *Kabuki* play at *Kabukiza Theatre* don't come with assigned seats, so it is recommended to arrive earlier to get a seat. We came at 10AM, and while there were many people in front of us, we got seats.

- If you are planning to go to a *Kabuki* play, I recommend getting a screen with subtitles when you purchase the tickets.

- I would suggest avoiding the lunch hour rush to have a more enjoyable experience at popular restaurants.

- Instead of traveling with your luggage between different cities, send it to your destination hotel with the luggage delivery service. Ask the front desk of your hotel for more information.

- If you intend to send luggage to a hotel, make sure to contact the hotel before doing so. Not all hotels may be able to accept deliveries due to lack of storage space[9].

- If you plan to visit Shinhotaka-ropeway, ask the reception clerk in your hotel whether there is fog there.

- It's recommended that you carry a bag with you wherever you go to avoid situations where you have something you need to dispose of but can't find a garbage bin around.

- If you plan to purchase a knife in Japan, I suggest doing some research online, so you can pick the knife that best suits your needs.

- When buying a knife in Japan, it is worth investing in a rust-resistant knife, since it is easiest to take care of. Simply wash and dry the knife after use, and it can last you for many years.

- If you are visiting Kiyomizudera temple with your significant other, the veranda offers a very romantic spot to look at the sunset.

- Buying wagyu beef from a butcher is way cheaper than eating it in a restaurant. Try finding an accommodation with a kitchen to enjoy a nice piece of wagyu beef on a budget. Better yet, I recommend Piece hostel. Even though the room is tiny, the location, staff, breakfast, and kitchen more than make up for it.

- Seemingly, Doguyasuji street does have a great selection of knives and reasonable prices, but I still recommend purchasing a knife in a smaller store where you can get a lot of attention and help. We purchased our knives at Hayakawa Hamonoten. Not only did we get the knives for a good price, but we also received a helpful shopping experience and a lesson for life.

- For a romantic destination, try getting to Namba parks before the sunset, since the park offers a nice view of the city, especially during twilight.

- For a more quiet and relaxing experience in Dotonbori street, the above ground restaurants and cafes offer somewhat of a break from the crowd.

- Going to Kuromon Ichiba fish market close to the opening hours (9AM) is highly recommended. The market is mostly empty, and the fish is exceptionally fresh and delicious.

- If you plan to withdraw money in Japan, check online if your credit/debit card can be used in a 7-Eleven ATM[10], since it is a big chain with many branches throughout Japan.

Sources:

[1] https://www.hospitalitynet.org/news/4070411.html

[2] https://www.ricksteves.com/travel-tips/sleeping-eating/reserve-accommodations

[3] https://www.easygojapan.com/rental/en/news/info_prepaid-sim.html

[4] http://www.jreast.co.jp/e/stations/

[5] https://stbooking.co/en/5663

[6] https://www.chowhound.com/post/japanese-slurp-noodles-789005

[7] https://backpackerlee.wordpress.com/2014/01/28/a-whole-latte-chaos-starbucks-at-shibuya/

[8] http://www.sentoguide.info/etiquette

[9] https://www.japan-guide.com/e/e2278.html

[10] https://www.sevenbank.co.jp/oos/adv/intlcard02/en/

18

Trip Budget

The list below summarizes how much money we spent on accommodations, transportation, food, and attractions during our trip to Japan. This list can give you an idea of how to plan your own budget.

NOTE: All prices are in JPY and per couple unless stated otherwise.

Accommodations:

Tokyo
   - Hotel Lungwood: approx. ¥9,550 per room per night.
   - Mystays hotel: about ¥9,500 per room per night.
   Average: ¥9,525 per room per night.

Hirayu
   - Nakamurakan Ryokan: ¥24,840 per room per night. This includes traditional dinner and breakfast).

Takayama
   - Country hotel: ¥6,800 per room per night.

Kyoto
   - New Piece hostel: about ¥10,200 per room per night.

Osaka
  - Teikoku hotel: ¥8,250 per room per night.
  - City Hotel Airport in Prince: ¥8,600 per room per night.
  Average: ¥8,367 per room per night.

Total accommodations cost for 14 days: ¥144,490.

Transportation:

Inside the city:

Tokyo: ¥5,000.
 Kyoto: ¥3,000.
 Osaka: ¥1,000.

Buses between cities:

Tokyo to Hirayu: ¥11,720.
 Round trip Hirayu to Kappabashi: ¥4,100.
 Hirayu to Takayama: ¥3,240.
 Round trip Takayama to Hida folk village: ¥1,860.
 Takayama to Kyoto: ¥8,400.

Total transportation for 14 days: ¥38,320.

Food:

We ate a lot of street food during our trip. Street food is considered less expensive than dining at restaurants. However, we also ate much more than we usually do, and we also enjoyed some expensive foods (such as wagyu beef).

Total average cost per day: ¥12,000.

Average cost per day in different cities:

Tokyo: ¥12,000.
Takayama: ¥9,500.
Kyoto: ¥13,000.
Osaka: ¥12,500.

*Note: the average cost does not include Hirayu.

Attractions:

- Purikura (photo booth). You can print two copies for ¥400.
    - Hamarikyu gardens: ¥300 entry fee per person.
    - Alice in fantasy book themed cafe: ¥500 entrance fee per person.
    - *Cat Cafe MoCHA:* ¥200 per every 10 minutes per person.
    - Saito-yu public bath: costs ¥430 per person.
    - A single act of a Kabuki play in Kabukiza Theatre: ¥1,500 per person.
    - Private outdoor bath: ¥1,000 per night.
    - Hida Folk Village: ¥700 entrance fee per person.
    - *Kinkakuji,* the gold Zen temple: ¥400 admission fee per person.
    Total attractions cost for 14 days: ¥10,260.

Other:

- 2GB SIM card that is active for 30 days costs ¥3,800.

19

What to Eat in Japan

We gathered a list of foods (and drinks) we suggest trying during your visit to Japan:

Must-try:

We chose to add the following items to the must-try list since we believe without them our food experience in Japan wouldn't be as great as it was. These are the items we enjoyed the most during our visit:

- **Yakitori:** Yakitori is a small skewer, that may be meat or vegetable, or both, cooked over a charcoal grill. Some examples: cherry tomato, green pepper, chicken breast, chicken skin, chicken liver, chicken thighs with leek, and chicken hearts.
- **Miso soup:** Miso soup is the fermented soul food of Japan, and often accompanies the main dish.
- **Street food**. Some examples: fried pastry filled with pork meat, crab leg on a stick.
- **Tempura:** Tempura is deep fried battered fish, seafood, or vegetable. Some examples: shrimp, white fish, eel, green beans, and yam. Worth trying in: *Tempura Tendon Tenya* restaurant (Day 2).
- **Ramen:** Ramen consists of noodles in a broth (fish, meat, or miso based) with a few toppings. Try it the Ramen Street in Tokyo station

(Day 4).

- **Sashimi:** Raw fish. Some examples: Tuna, Salmon, prawns, and Mackerel.

- **Nigiri:** Fish over rice, with a bit of wasabi in between. Some examples: Tuna, Salmon, Squid, eel, raw sweet shrimp, and Wagyu beef. Worth trying in: Kuromon Ichiba market (day 14).

- *Chirashizushi:* Chirashizushi is a bowl of rice, topped with a variety of sashimi. Worth trying in: *Sushi Tomi* restaurant (Day 4).

- **EEl.** Worth trying in: *Sukiya* restaurant (Day 6), or *Unashin* restaurant (Day 9).

- **Japanese beef curry**. Worth trying in: *Sukiya* restaurant (Day 6).

- **Udon:** Udon soup is soup with thick noodles made from wheat flour. Udon noodles are very popular in Japan and can also be served chilled with a dipping sauce[1]. Worth trying in: *Yoshimoto* restaurant (Day 8), or in Tanimachi-suji street in Osaka (Day 13).

- *Uni:* Uni is a sea urchin. Worth trying in: Nishiki market (Day 11).

- **Fresh oysters**. Worth trying in: Nishiki market (Day 11).

- **Steamed bun filled with pork meat:** The steamed dough is very soft and airy, while the pork meat inside is hot and juicy.

- **Crab miso:** Crab miso is creamy crab meat with miso topped with green onion slices, inside a crab shell. You heat it on a grill until this crab shell full of goodness sizzles. Worth trying in *Isomaru Suisan* restaurant (Day 2 or day 12).

- *Gyoza:* Gyoza is a Japanese dumpling usually filled with pork meat, steamed, and fried on one side until crispy brown. This process makes the meat inside very juicy, while the dough becomes slightly sweet from the frying. Worth trying in: *Harajuku Gyouzarou* restaurant in Tokyo (Day 5) or Osaka Ohsho in Osaka (Day 14).

- **Wagyu beef:** Wagyu beef is a sort of beef cattle that originated in Japan. Compared to regular beef, Wagyu beef has more fat inside their muscles, which provides the meat a marbled look and great texture. Worth trying in: *Tenaga Ashinaga Hommachi* restaurant (Day 8) or Mitsuru restaurant (Day 14).

Sweets:

- **Japanese crepe:** Crepes filled with fruits, ice cream, chocolates, and more sweets. Worth trying in: *Takeshita Dori* street (Day 5).
- ***CROQUANT CHOU:*** CROQUANT CHOU is a warm and crunchy cream puff with a sweet filling. Worth trying in: *Takeshita Dori* street (Day 5).
- **Ice cream.** Some examples: black sesame, Sakura, matcha, and ice cream with soy sauce.
- **Mochi ice cream.** You can buy it in a grocery store.
- **Fish shaped pastries:** Fish shaped pastries come with a variety of stuffing, including green tea, custard, and red beans. Worth trying in: Takayama morning market (Day 9).
- ***Kakigōri:*** Kakigōri is a Japanese dessert that consists of shaved ice topped with a sweet syrup, and sometimes condensed milk.
- **Baked Melon-pan Ice cream.** Worth trying in Dotonbori (Day 14).

Drinks:

- **Japanese whiskey.** Worth trying: Yamazaki Single Malt Sherry Cask 2013.
- **Sake:** Sake is the national beverage, made from fermented rice, water, koji mold, and yeast[2]. Some examples: Kokuryu, Dassai, Hakkaisan, and Tozai.
- **Coffee in a can:** Some vending machines offer hot coffee. Make sure there is a sign that says the drinks are hot.
- **Matcha tea:** Matcha tea is a tea made of ground green tea leaves. Worth trying in: a tea house in the gardens of the golden pavilion in Kyoto (Day 11).
- **Hand drip coffee:** Hand drip coffee also known as *pour-over* coffee. Worth trying in: Elephant Factory Coffee in Kyoto (Day 11).
- ***Siphon* coffee:** Syphon coffee is a type of coffee that is made in many cafes in Japan.
- **Japanese beer.** Some examples: Asahi, Kirin, and Sapporo.

- **Plum liqueur:** Sweet and sour liqueur with 10-15% alcohol.

Worth trying:

The following items didn't reach our *Must-try* list. However, we do suggest trying them if you get a chance.

- **Traditional *bento box*:** Bento box is a meal packed in a box. The traditional variation often offers rice or noodles, fish or meat, and pickled and cooked vegetables.

- ***Ganmodoki*:** Ganmodoki is a Japanese fritter made of tofu and vegetables and soaked in broth.

- **Marinated mackerel:** Mackerel is one of the favorite fish in Japan.

- **Oden:** Oden is a warm dish that includes many different ingredients, simmered in a broth. Each ingredient is ordered by the piece and served inside the broth. Some examples: shrimp cutlets, quail eggs, and radish. Worth trying in: *Otafuku* restaurant (Day 2).

- ***Senbei*:** Senbei are rice crackers. They come in many shapes and flavors. You can buy it in a grocery store, or from speciality shops.

- ***Korokke*:** Korokke is a croquette. Try it filled with Japanese curry in the Nippori train station.

- **Japanese omelet**.

- ***Soba* noodles:** Soba noodles are thin noodles made from buckwheat flour, and could either be served warm or cold. Worth trying in: *Yoshimoto* restaurant (Day 8).

- ***Tonkatsu*:** Tonkatsu is a deep-fried breaded pork, served with shredded cabbage, and a Tonkatsu sauce. Worth trying in: <u>Nishimura</u> restaurant (Day 6).

- ***Onigiri*:** Onigiri is a rice ball (or triangle) wrapped with seaweed, with different fillings. You can buy it in a grocery store.

- ***Kaiseki* dinner:** A kaiseki dinner is a multi-course traditional Japanese dinner. It contains some standard components: an appetizer (*Sakizuze*), seasonal sashimi (*Mukōzuke*), a dish with a lid (*Futamono*), pickled vegetables (*Kō no mono*), miso soup, and dessert (*Mizumono*)[3].

- **_Natto:_** Natto is a dish made of fermented soybeans. It has a very pungent smell, a strong flavor, and a slimy texture.

- **_Okonomiyaki:_** Okonomiyaki is a pan-fried pancake made of batter, cabbage, and a variation of additional ingredients and toppings[4].

- **Hida beef sushi:** Hida beef sushi is made from a lightly seared Hida beef, and might be topped with a quail egg yolk. Worth trying in: Kotte gyu, in the old town of Takayama (Day 9).

- **Roast beef and steak bowls.** Worth trying in: Red Rock restaurant in Kyoto (Day 9).

- **_Inarizushi:_** Inarizushi is a deep-fried tofu in a pocket shape, filled with rice[5].

- **_Takoyaki:_** Takoyaki is a ball-shaped pancake, filled with octopus (tako)[6]. Worth trying in: the golden pavilion bus stop (Day 11), or in Dotonbori (Day 12).

- **_Surimi_ fish cakes:** Surimi fish cakes are made of ground fish. By adjusting their shape and texture, they are used to mimic the taste of lobster, crab, or other shellfish[7]. Worth trying in: Nishiki market (Day 11).

- **_Kushikatsu:_** Kushikatsu is battered and deep-fried meat, seafood, or vegetable skewers[9].

Sources:

[1] https://www.japan-talk.com/jt/new/japanese-food-list

[2] http://www.japan-guide.com/e/e2037_sake.html

[3] https://en.wikipedia.org/wiki/Kaiseki

[4] https://www.japan-guide.com/r/e100.html

[5]https://gurunavi.com/en/japanfoodie/2017/10/a-guide-to-inarizushi-japans-sweet-sushi-tofu-pockets.html?___ngt___ =TT0df24d0c7001ac1e4ae862GzRwn43IRrpDnj75veGfdf

[6] https://en.wikipedia.org/wiki/Takoyaki

[7] https://en.wikipedia.org/wiki/Surimi

[8] https://savorjapan.com/contents/more-to-savor/eating-fugu-the-deadly-and-delicious-japanese-pufferfish/

[9] https://www.tsunagujapan.com/the-right-way-to-eat-the-famous-osaka-kushikatsu/

20

What to Buy in Japan

The following list contains information about items that are unique to Japan, and are worth buying in Japan.

*Note: make sure to check customs regulations and airline guidelines before bringing Japanese souvenirs on the plane with you.

Japanese whiskey: Japanese whiskey is so good, that in 2014 Yamazaki Single Malt Sherry Cask 2013 won the world's best whiskey title[1]. A few more whiskey brands worth exploring in Japan can be found here: www.gq.com

Sake: Sake is the national drink in Japan. Takayama has many sake breweries, and the sake produced there are considered some of the best in Japan[2]. Some people travel to Takayama for a sake tour during mid-January to late February, when a few of the breweries open their doors to the public (day 8).

Food items:

- Green tea: Tea, and green tea in particular, are a significant part of the Japanese food culture[3]. There are many different kinds of green tea sold in supermarkets, specialty stores, or even in souvenir shops.

- Matcha: Matcha is made out of ground green tea leaves. It is served in tea ceremonies[4]. To prepare matcha, you need a whisk and a bowl. These items can also be purchased throughout Japan.

- Miso: Miso is fermented soybeans. It has long been a staple food in the Japanese kitchen and is the main ingredient of miso soup.

- KitKats: There are many limited edition KitKat varieties that are solely sold in Japan[5].
- Savory lollipops: Japan has many unique lollipop flavors. Some examples include: Ramen flavor and salted plum.
- Rice crackers: Rice crackers, or *senbei*, are crunchy crackers made of a non-sticky rice dough[6]. There are many varieties of rice crackers in Japan, many of them are simply delicious.

Toilet seat. The interesting thing about the toilet seats in Japan is how advanced they are. Common features include seat warmer, and front and back washing hoses. They have a control that contains many buttons that offer different functions. Some people like the toilet seats in Japan so much, that they buy several to bring home with them[7]. There are a few things worth checking in advance: do they comply with the voltage and toilet shape of your home country? We decided not to buy the toilet seat in Japan, but we definitely were tempted by it.

Accessories/jewelry:
- *Kanzashi*, an ornamental hair stick: It is a great part of the Japanese history and culture. Nowadays, Kanzashi is mainly worn by brides, geishas, maikos, or by adepts in a tea ceremony, however some young women wear it as a fashion statement.
- Flower hairpins: Wearing flowers in your hair is very popular in Japan. Not only that it is popular, but it is also very pretty.

Souvenirs: Different regions in Japan have unique souvenirs, for example, Sarubobo doll in the Hida region. These souvenirs can be purchased in the region they are coming from. They can also be purchased in various Antenna Shops in Tokyo.

Kitchen items:
- Japanese knives: Knives in Japan are considered the highest quality in the world.
- Hand drip coffee filter cone and filters: All the necessities for making a great hand drip coffee can be purchased in Japan.
- *Kyo-yaki*: Kyo-Yaki is pottery made in Kyoto, and it dates back to the 16th century.

Art: Japanese art is both esthetic and of high quality. Some examples include: a woodblock print, paintings, and printed textiles.

Sources:

[1]https://www.washingtonpost.com/news/morning-mix/wp/2014/11/05/japan-beats-scotland-to-win-worlds-best-whiskey-title/?noredirect=on&utm_term=.6a2d97956154

[2] https://samuraitrip.com/en/takayama/articles/sake-breweries-takayama

[3] https://www.japan-guide.com/e/e2041.html

[4] https://www.japan-guide.com/e/e2041.html

[5] https://en.wikipedia.org/wiki/Kit_Kats_in_Japan

[6] https://matcha-jp.com/en/2024

[7]https://www.tripadvisor.ca/ShowTopic-g298184-i861-k7559788-My_crazy_souvenir_quest_magical_Japanese_toilet_seat-Tokyo_Tokyo_Prefecture_Kanto.html

57983344R00126

Made in the USA
Middletown, DE
03 August 2019